What Do We Know About Jesus?

What Do We Know About Jesus?

OTTO BETZ

THE WESTMINSTER PRESS
PHILADELPHIA

© SCM PRESS Ltd. 1968

Translated by Margaret Kohl from the German *Was wissen wir von Jesus?* published 1965 by Kreuz-Verlag, Stuttgart.

LIBRARY OF CONGRESS CATALOG CARD NO. 68–18938

Published by The Westminster Press ®
Philadelphia, Pennsylvania

PRINTED IN THE UNITED STATES OF AMERICA

CONTENTS

6　　　　　　　　　　*Contents*

FOREWORD

CRITICAL WORK on the New Testament continually confronts us with the challenging question of the historical basis of our faith. Is there a bedrock of fact, untouched by the breakers of doubt and impregnable to the flood of ever-new theories? What do we really know about Jesus?

This book provides an answer – though admittedly an incomplete one – to this question. It rejects the view that the Gospels are not intended to stand up to historical investigation. It is true that they are designed to be read as a testimony of faith, not as historical sources. But each of the four Gospels paints a picture of Jesus as a historical figure. If these pictures are compared, both similarities and dissimilarities emerge. For this reason alone, the Gospels force us to make our own picture of Jesus, one which will do justice both to their testimony and to our own restless urge for truth.

This is admittedly a task in which we are constantly going astray and which cannot therefore be completed at all in this world. Research will never arrive once and for all at the historical Jesus. But the historical Jesus is none the less open to research. An *a priori* 'no' is as inadmissible here as it would be in the case of, for example, the historical Moses or the historical Socrates.

The progress of scholarship and the extension of our historical horizon demands the constant revision and voluntary alteration of our picture of the Jesus of history. In this process we may be occasionally helped by an unexpected event. I am here thinking of the Dead Sea Scrolls, which a fortunate chance presented to us a few years ago. The teachings contained in these writings form a highly important background to the following discussion. The Dead Sea Scrolls were compiled by the Essenes, a sect which was widespread in Palestine at the time of Jesus. Their founder, the 'Teacher of Righteousness', probably lived about a hundred years before Jesus was born. Geographically and spiritually the Essenes were centred on a desert monastery not far from Jericho; its ruins, which can still be seen today, bear the name Khirbet Qumran. Of the manuscripts which are mentioned below, the Manual of Discipline or Community Rule (1QS) and its supplement (1QSa), with the Damascus Rule (CD), primarily contain the rules for the communal life of the Essenes. The religious attitude of the group is reflected particularly in the Thanksgiving Hymns (1QH), and their eschatological expectations in the War Rule (1QM) as well as in the Commentary on the Book of Habakkuk (1QpHab) and in the 'Book of Mysteries' (1Q27).

1

THE PROBLEM OF THE HISTORICAL JESUS

The Proclamation of Faith and the Historical Facts

IN 1904 an essay by Wilhelm Bousset was published under the title 'What do we know about Jesus?'. It was at this time that the dispute about the 'Christ myth' had arisen. People such as Kalthoff, Drews or Jensen had maintained that there had never been a real Jesus of Nazareth and that the basis of the Christ of the New Testament was a mythical, supra-historical figure to whom Christians had subsequently given a time and place, thus artificially historicizing him. It was not difficult for New Testament scholars like Bousset, Jülicher or Klostermann to expose the 'Christ myth' as a phantom, and since that time no serious scholar has ventured to postulate the non-historicity of Jesus.

Even non-Christian sources permit no doubt as to the actual existence of Jesus of Nazareth. It is true that these sources are few and far between and that the earliest were compiled about two generations after Jesus' death. In his *Jewish Antiquities* Josephus describes James, who was stoned to death in AD 62, as 'the brother of Jesus, the so-called Christ'.[1] This note suggests that the Jewish historian had already spoken of Jesus earlier and was therefore

[1] 20.200. The *Jewish Antiquities*, Josephus' most extensive work, were completed in AD 93. A convenient translation of the passage can be found in C. K. Barrett, *The New Testament Background: Selected Documents*, London 1956, pp. 199 f.

assuming that the name would be familiar to his readers. In fact, in the eighteenth book of the *Antiquities* we find the famous *Testimonium Flavianum*, the testimony of Flavius Josephus to Christ, though this is no longer in its original form but must have been revised by a Christian hand.[2] It is nevertheless quite possible that at this point Josephus spoke of Jesus as a wise teacher and miracle-worker, who was denounced to Pilate by the Jewish authorities because of his messianic claims and was crucified on Pilate's orders. A little later Tacitus traces the name 'Christians' to the founder of the sect, Christ, who was executed on Pilate's orders under the Emperor Tiberius.[3] According to Suetonius, the Emperor Claudius (AD 41-54) banished the Jews from Rome because 'at the instigation of Chrestus[4] they created constant unrest'.[5] 'Chrestus' doubtless means Christ, and Suetonius' remark may refer to disturbances due to Christian-Jewish tension; though apparently Suetonius had only a vague notion of the actual facts. In a letter to the Emperor Trajan, the Roman governor Pliny the Younger reports that the Christians used to sing a hymn to Christ as to a God.[6] The few, mostly obscure, passages in the Talmud where Jesus is mentioned speak of him as an illegitimate child, a miracle-worker, sorcerer and heretical teacher, who was hanged on the eve of the feast of the Passover.[7] These statements reveal

[2] It seems unjustifiable to regard the whole *Testimonium Flavianum* (*Antiquities*, 18.63-64) as a Christian insertion. Quoted in Barrett, op. cit., pp. 198 f.

[3] *Annals* 15.44; this work was written in AD 112-3. Quoted in J. Stevenson, *A New Eusebius*, London 1957, p. 2.

[4] '*Chresto impulsore*'.

[5] *Claudius* 25. The Lives of the Emperors were written in AD 121. It is worth comparing Acts 18.2 with this edict. Cf. Stevenson, op. cit., p. 1, for the passage.

[6] *Letters* 10.96, written in AD 112. Quoted in Stevenson, op. cit., p. 14.

[7] These passages are quoted with critical comments in J. Klausner, *Jesus of Nazareth*, New York 1926, pp. 17-56.

little historical knowledge, replacing it by frequently violent polemic; but they indicate no doubt whatever about the genuine existence of Jesus.

The most important source for our knowledge of Jesus thus remains the New Testament writings, especially the Gospels. No one who reads these objectively can doubt that here, too, a real historical personage is being described. But the Gospels are fundamentally different from the references to Jesus we have noted in Tacitus, Josephus or the Talmud. The evangelists wrote detailed accounts of Jesus – indeed he is their sole subject. More important still, they saw him from a completely different point of view. For them Jesus was not a justly executed heretic, magical miracle-worker or revolutionary; he was the Messiah, who proclaimed the coming of the kingdom of God, healed the sick, died innocently on the cross and was therefore raised by God to life again. Their account is shaped by their belief in Jesus as Christ; the earthly Jesus of Nazareth is equated with the risen and glorified Lord of Christendom. The evangelists, writing forty to fifty years after Jesus' death, stand in a double relationship to him – both horizontal and vertical: on the one hand through the current of tradition, which carried the words and acts of the earthly Jesus to them; on the other through faith in the heavenly Christ, present in the preached word, in the Holy Spirit and in the sacraments. The modern distinction between Jesus as a historical figure and Christ as a historical force did not exist for them. For even the store of tradition about the earthly Jesus was frequently coloured by belief in the Christ. Carried by the wings of faith over the sea of time, the Jesus of tradition reached the evangelists with the familiar features of the Christ and Son of God. Each of the Gospels is therefore characterized by its particular christology.

The historical enquirer is consequently faced with severe

difficulties. A Christ and Son of God goes far beyond the bounds of what we can know about a historical figure; it is part of the realm of faith, of creeds and dogmas. The historian asks himself whether the glorified Lord of the church can be brought down to earth and the bedrock of historical fact again – whether it is possible to strip away the gold of the icon in order to reveal the figure of the man, Jesus of Nazareth, as he really was. Is it methodologically possible to arrive at the Jesus of history on the basis of the Gospels, dominated as they are by faith in Christ? If the answer is 'yes', the theologian is bound to ask whether the church, which calls itself Christian and stands or falls by its belief in Christ as Son of God, really needs to know about the historical Jesus of Nazareth, the teacher, miracle-worker, revolutionary, or whatever he may have been.

Rudolf Bultmann's answer is a flat 'no'. In his view the quest for the historical Jesus is methodologically doomed to failure and is, in any case, from the point of view of faith, illegitimate. This quest, so magisterially described by Albert Schweitzer, shows that a 'Life', a biography, of the man Jesus of Nazareth cannot be written at all in academically acceptable form. That is basically due to the nature of the sources. A Gospel is not designed to be a life-history of a famous man and consequently it does not offer data for an unimpeachable biography. Bultmann maintains that the historical enquirer cannot, even from these detailed sources, derive more than the bare 'that' of existence – the fact that a man called Jesus of Nazareth really lived. But the church, which lives by faith in Christ, needs no more than this basic fact, that Jesus was a person belonging to history and hence more than a mere symbol or mythical figure. For true faith will not rest on scientifically established, universally acceptable facts. It clings to the Word of God, which is outside human control. It is this Word alone, proclaimed by the New

Testament church, which leads us to the crucified and risen Lord. The statement that Jesus of Nazareth is the Christ, the saviour of mankind, cannot be demonstrated as a general and inevitable truth. It only becomes true in the venture of faith, the venture of a free, personal decision. There can be no doubt that with this Bultmann has rightly discerned the nature of the Gospels and the essence of Christian faith. 'Gospel' means good news, a testimony glowing with faith and demanding faith in return, calling a man in question, pointing him in a new direction; it is not an invitation to a coldly scientific examination and rendition.

Yet Bultmann's 'no' to the Jesus of history is not satisfactory. True, faith in Christ cannot be based on historical facts. But if faith is directed towards a person who appears in history, in time and space, then the historical facts cannot be a matter of indifference. The mere existence of the Gospels is sufficient evidence of that. They do not only show, as Paul does for example, the crucified and risen Christ; they go behind the cross and report the words and works of the earthly Jesus of Nazareth. This was certainly not merely for the sake of edification. The second generation of Christians was already filled with anxiety about the truth, the historical basis, of their preaching. They were fighting on two different fronts: against the Jews, to whom the reality of God's power in the sphere of history had been revealed and who thus thought and questioned in historical terms; and on the other hand against gnosticism, an ever-increasing heresy within the church in which the historical facts evaporated and the humanity of Jesus was denied. In addition, there was the fact that with the fall of Jerusalem in AD 70 the church was robbed of its historical centre and had therefore reason to be particularly concerned with the protection of its tradition. In this situation the question of who Jesus of Nazareth really was and what the individual Christian or

Jew thought of him could no longer remain a matter of indifference.

This basically applies to Bultmann too. In apparent contradiction to his own veto, he has published a book, *Jesus*,[8] which has received much attention; significantly, the English edition is entitled *Jesus and the Word*. In this book Jesus is presented as a rabbinical teacher and prophetic herald who, through his proclamation of the kingdom of God, confronted men with the will of God, interpreted radically. Jesus summoned his hearers to a life not based upon the readily available but transitory goods and values of this world; he urged them to see themselves instead in the light of the higher reality of God and to accept the true existence of faith, free for neighbourly love.

Bultmann crystallized Jesus' message out of the Gospels with the help of form-critical methods. The form critic tries to get behind the present form of the Gospels, seeking thus the way to the historical Jesus. He examines the pre-literary 'forms', the tiny units of oral tradition – parables and miracles, wisdom sayings and prophetic words, legal precepts and 'apophthegmata', i.e., short, anecdotal scenes crowned by a saying of Jesus. When the typical form or 'Gattung' of such a unit has been grasped, its *Sitz im Leben*, or 'situation', can usually also be determined; for example, while the parable belongs to Jesus' preaching about the kingdom of God, the legal precepts may more probably derive from the life and rule of the Christian community; the former may be a genuine saying of Jesus, while the latter may be a formulation of the early church. When the whole of a Gospel has been dissected in this way, a constructive attempt can be made to trace the evolution of the Jesus-tradition and to describe its historical growth and the tendencies that have

---

[8] German original: Rudolf Bultmann, *Jesus*, Tübingen 1951; English version: *Jesus and the Word*, Fontana Books 1958.

determined it. In the opinion of Bultmann and his pupils it emerges that a large part of the Gospel material can be attributed to Jesus' disciples, the church. Everything that the New Testament tells us of Jesus went through the medium of the church which, according to Bultmann, was by no means content with the role of conscientious transmitter. On the contrary, the judicial use of form-critical analysis gives the impression that the Christian community built up its belief in the risen Lord with an elemental creative power and in the course of so doing also shaped and developed the Jesus-tradition along the same lines. It did not only view the acts of Jesus in the light of Easter and its faith in Christ; it also mixed up the words of the risen Lord, proclaimed by inspired prophets, with those of the earthly Jesus.

In the end, no definite conclusion emerges. Consequently, in *Jesus and the Word*, Bultmann does not draw a hard and fast line, taking over material which he really suggests is the work of the church. Form criticism leads him to the workshop of the church but not to the historical Jesus. Nor is this its purpose. Any book on Jesus designed only to depict the man of Nazareth would, according to Bultmann, be the work of a sceptic.

Bultmann's 'no' to the historical Jesus was greeted with disapproval by many New Testament scholars, especially in England, Scandinavia, America and Germany. Even Bultmann's own followers have abandoned this view since Käsemann's epoch-making essay 'The Problem of the Historical Jesus'.[9] Indeed this problem has become one of the most important subjects of New Testament research;[10] the 'new quest of the historical Jesus' ('new' to distinguish it from the liberal research of the last century) has been welcomed

[9] In *Essays on New Testament Themes*, London 1964, pp. 15-47.
[10] J. M. Robinson, 'The Formal Structure of Jesus' Message', in *Current Issues in New Testament Interpretation*, ed. W. Klassen and G. F. Snyder, London and New York 1962, p. 91.

enthusiastically, particularly in America. Admittedly, there, too, critical voices can be heard. It is said that the 'new quest' hardly goes further than Bultmann and that where it does it falls into the psychologizing attitude of the liberals.[11]

Is this criticism justified? How new is the 'new quest' in actual point of fact? There is no doubt that Bultmann's followers are still under the spell of their master and adhere to his theology. It is still the church's proclamation of Christ towards which faith is directed, not Jesus' preaching or his own sense of mission. It is at this point above all that the 'new quest' diverges radically from the Jesus-research of the liberal period. But it is stressed that the connection between the message of the church and the preaching of Jesus is by no means insignificant, quite apart from the fact that no scholar allows limits to be set beyond which he may not go. Form-critical evidence, applied with 'methodological scepticism',[12] still remains the most important instrument of research on the Gospels. But this research has now taken a new turn. With Bultmann the form-critical method had primarily a critical force. Naïve trust in the Gospels as a historical account was shattered and the false supports of faith collapsed; in this process access to the historical Jesus was blocked rather than opened up. Bultmann's followers still delight in practising the art of criticism, especially when the object is the destruction of the hypotheses of other theologians and the nowadays so-conservative liberal scholars. But they have a positive aim which is still more important to them – a return to the genuine words of Jesus. The preaching of Jesus now acquires an intrinsic value. It is no

[11] Van A. Harvey and Schubert M. Ogden, 'How new is the "New Quest of the Historical Jesus"?', in *The Historical Jesus and the Kerygmatic Christ*, ed. Carl E. Braaten and Roy A. Harrisville, Nashville 1964, pp. 197-242.
[12] This is the way in which Hans Conzelmann describes the critical force of the form-critical method in 'Jesus', *Die Religion in Geschichte und Gegenwart*[3], III, col. 620.

longer, as in Bultmann, merely the presupposition of the *kerygma*, of New Testament theology;[13] it is its foundation. If the church's message of Christ is to escape exposure as a pure soliloquy, it needs support in history – the pointer to the *extra nos* of salvation.[14] Through the teaching and person of Jesus of Nazareth, faith in Christ, the saviour of the world, possesses this historical foundation. Thus the Christian proclamation stands on firm ground and is prevented from becoming an arbitrary, insubstantial, mythological construction. Continuity is of decisive importance: it is a question of showing that the church's faith in Christ is the proper response not only to the events of Easter but also to Jesus' preaching. Hence the authenticity of every piece of tradition must be tested and made convincing.[15]

The result of the 'new quest' is also more positive, the broad, ugly cleft in Bultmann between Jesus' teaching and the proclamation of Christ seeming less wide. Bultmann gives the impression that Jesus neither preached nor believed anything specifically Christian. Wellhausen's remark that Jesus was the last of the Jews and Paul the first Christian could be Bultmann's: Jesus belonged to late Judaism, while Christ was first recognized and confessed by the primitive church. At Easter he was elevated into a *kerygma*, and proclaimed as Messiah by the disciples, whose faith spread ever-widening circles of believing praise round the risen Lord. Bultmann's followers also stress increasingly the original and unique quality of Jesus' words and works. Where Bultmann saw in Jesus the rabbinical teacher of a radically interpreted Law, Käsemann brings to the fore the contrast between Jesus and contemporary Judaism – the unprecedented sovereignty with which he could by-pass the

[13] *Theology of the New Testament*, Vol. 1, London and New York 1952, p. 3.
[14] E. Käsemann, 'The Problem of the Historical Jesus', in *Essays on New Testament Themes*, London 1964, p. 33.   [15] Ibid., p. 34.

letter of the Torah and the authority of Moses, and his joyous message of the graciousness of the heavenly Father and the freedom of the children of God.[16]

Yet even the 'new quest of the historical Jesus' gives the impression of being constricted, both for dogmatic reasons and because it binds itself too exclusively to the methods of form criticism. The reserve in the face of historical and objective facts, which was inoculated by Bultmann, has by no means disappeared. Archaeological data – inscriptions, coins, buildings, even the Dead Sea Scrolls – receive only limited attention. The main stress lies on the message of Jesus and the faith which both witnesses to it and liberates it; everything else is labelled 'milieu' and is of only secondary importance. But a division of this kind (influenced by the philosophy of Heidegger or Collingwood) makes it all too easy to forget that the search for the Jesus of history cannot be confined to theological or philosophical questions. Everything is of interest to the historian, not only the world of ideas, in which the subjective viewpoint plays a part, but every detail of the 'milieu' as well. Before he preaches what Jesus 'brings to expression' he considers the language used by Jesus and concerns himself with its details. Before he declares a credal formulation to be Palestinian or Hellenistic, he thinks back to its Hebraic, Aramaic or Greek form. And how can one understand the 'inner life' of a historical figure without taking note of his environment, the field within which he works? The environment is especially important when the scholar is separated from the subject of his account by a wide temporal and spatial gap. The 'new quest' therefore leaves a divided impression: the wall between the proclaimed Christ and the historical Jesus has been broken down, but the field that lies behind the wall is being traversed with half-closed eyes.

"New quest" - too limited scope.

16 Ibid., pp. 38-44.

This constraint is further conditioned by the fact that form criticism is the one accepted method. It is not our intention to belittle the value of form criticism. It illuminates, for example, the various tendencies which determine the features of the Gospels: belief in the Son of God, whose divine power was mysteriously revealed even in his earthly activity (Mark); the missionary zeal which was to open the way for the message of Christ in Judaism and beyond, to the whole world (Matthew); the apologetic purpose of justifying the sincerity of Jesus before the Roman authorities (Luke). Form criticism leads to an older, less distorted layer of the Jesus-tradition. But did the church really have a creative influence to the extent that Bultmann's analysis suggests? Did it not rather make a selection from the material at its disposal and give this a form in line with its own concerns? Is the outline of the activity of Jesus given first by Mark and then largely taken over by Matthew and Luke simply a free invention? Does it not in fact follow the stages of Jesus' life?[17] The 'methodological scepticism' with which form criticism is to be applied would seem to be by no means infallible and calls in its turn for a sceptically critical eye. Its insufficiency is shown merely by the fact that there are quite different judgments among form critics about the authenticity of any given saying of Jesus. Even in the ranks of Bultmann's own followers there is anything but general agreement. On the contrary, there are the most violent disputes among them, in the course of which many a form-critical judgment as to the genuineness of a particular passage falls a victim to an acuter logic.[18]

[17] See T. W. Manson, *Studies in the Gospels and Epistles*, edited by Matthew Black, Manchester 1962, pp. 5 f., 26.

[18] See especially P. Vielhauer's criticism of the position of E. Schweizer, H. E. Tödt and Ferdinand Hahn in 'Jesus und der Menschensohn', *Zeitschrift für Theologie und Kirche* 60 (1963), pp. 133-77.

The fact that form-critical methods alone do not make it possible to separate with certainty a genuine saying of Jesus from a later invention of the Christian community can be explained by the similarity of the '*Sitz im Leben*' in both cases – i.e., the situation for which such a saying was coined. Both Jesus and the first Christians were influenced by eschatological expectations; both preached the coming of the kingdom of God, the resurrection of the dead and the Last Judgment. And both saw the eschatological activity of God, and the repentance of man which it demanded, in the light of the Old Testament message. Further, it must be remembered that our knowledge of the faith and hope, of the services and outward order, of the earliest Christian communities is full of gaps. If we attempt to expand our knowledge with the help of material sifted out of the Gospels and Pauline epistles by means of form-critical distinctions, we are inevitably involved in a methodological circle: a measuring-rod is already being made of the very thing which it is the object of research to establish.

In the judgment of the Bultmann school genuine sayings of Jesus must be clearly distinguishable, not only from the spirit and order of the Christian community but also from the thought of contemporary Judaism; there must be no rabbinic parallels. This criterion also seems a doubtful one; for if the fact that Jesus was a Jew and 'a servant to the circumcised' (Rom. 15.8) is taken seriously, it must be readily accepted that he would share words and ideas which were common to his people or were also taught by other devout men of his time.

Notable objections to form criticism and the scepticism that goes with it are at present being made by the Scandinavian New Testament scholars Harald Riesenfeld[19] and

[19] *The Gospel Tradition and Its Beginnings. A Study in the Limits of 'Formgeschichte'*, London 1957.

Birger Gerhardsson.[20] In their opinion the New Testament tradition must be viewed in the light of the activity of Jewish schools at the time of Jesus. The rabbis were scrupulously concerned to see that their teaching was passed down word for word. Consequently they put their precepts into memorable form and had them repeated with rigid accuracy by their scholars; occasional written notes were also made. The saying was: 'The man who repeats his chapter one hundred times is not to be compared with the man who repeats it one hundred and one times.'[21] The pupil revered the teacher as the bearer of the tradition received on Sinai; he therefore took pains to engrave the teaching word for word on his memory, thus making himself a link in the chain of transmission. In the judgment of the two Scandinavian scholars, the Jesus-tradition followed similar rules. It was stamped on the memory from the beginning, sometimes being given a deliberately rhythmical and thus easily memorized form; it counted as 'the sacred Word'. What the disciples learnt at Jesus' feet was later solemnly recited in the services of the church. As the words of Christ, the redeemer of 'the latter days' and the second Moses, the tradition had among Christians the place which in rabbinic circles was held by the oral tradition going back to Sinai, or indeed by the written Law itself.

These points merit the greatest attention. But the conclusions drawn from them would seem to go too far. For, side by side with this faithfulness to tradition, applied according to rule, there are also signs of creative freedom. Even in the desert monastery of Qumran, of which we shall hear more later, there were several versions of important writings and these certainly betray no slavish attachment to the material

[20] *Memory and Manuscript. Oral Tradition and Written Transmission in Rabbinic Judaism and Early Christianity*, Uppsala 1961.
[21] Babylonian Talmud, *Ḥagiga* 9b, quoted in Gerhardsson, op. cit., p. 134.

as it had been passed down. In the Mishnah, a legal definition is sometimes repeated in another context; it may be
supplied with additional matter there or even formulated in
a different way. In the Talmud, of course, shorter or longer
pieces of tradition can appear in another context in almost
the same words, but they can also differ in detail and be
narrated quite freely. At the same time, however, the degree
of faithfulness to the tradition is indicated by the fact that
the final redactor of the Mishnah did not even venture to
remove obvious contradictions. The New Testament also
shows both facets – faithfulness to oral tradition and the
freedom of the evangelists in their use of it. What speaks for
the reliability of the tradition is, first, that in the few places
where Paul refers to a saying of the Lord a similar saying is
to be found in the Synoptic Gospels;[22] and, further, the
apostle makes a clear distinction between his own opinion
and a saying of the Lord which has been passed down (I
Cor. 7.10-11; 7.25). Mark tells stories that are similar to one
another in an almost stereotyped form; he avoids variety,
probably because he is anxiously clinging to oral tradition.[23]
As is well known, Matthew and Luke supplemented the
material taken over from Mark with additional matter,
largely sayings of Jesus. It is generally assumed that they
had an additional common source or *Ur*-Gospel, the so-
called 'Q'. But the way in which both of them use this non-
Marcan material suggests rather that they were able to draw
on a reservoir of oral tradition.[24] The transmission was
exact, but the evangelists ordered, interwove and sometimes
also interpreted the material in varying ways. Paul's conversion on the Damascus road is related three times in

[22] Compare I Cor. 7.10 f. with Matt. 5.32; I Cor. 9.14 with Luke
10.7; I Cor. 11.23-25 with Mark 14.22-24.
[23] R. M. Grant, *A Historical Introduction to the New Testament*,
London and New York 1963, p. 124.
[24] Ibid., pp. 115 f.

Acts.[25] Luke has no intention of repeating it mechanically word for word. He varies the details, leaving something out here, adding something new there, in order to fit the story better into the varying framework, but the essential content of what is being said remains the same in all three cases.

It is advisable, when considering both the New Testament writings and the problem of the historical Jesus, to trace the thinking of late Judaism and not simply to follow the laws of modern logic. The most important prolegomena to the Jesus of history was written by the Judaism of his own time. The Old Testament is basic for the understanding of Jesus. The disciples and Jesus himself, like the Pharisees, the Essenes and the Zealots, lived in the Old Testament. It was the Book of Books; God himself spoke to them through the lips of Moses and the prophets, all the more so because in the view of the majority the Holy Spirit and the word of the prophets had ceased to be actively revelatory in the present. The fact that the Jews in the Hellenistic and Roman period came into contact with other peoples, thereby widening their horizon, did not impair the authority of the Scriptures. On the contrary, an attempt was now made to give the Torah a universal significance and to see in it the basic law governing and binding together heaven and earth. At the time of Jesus it was considered to be not only instruction for the good life but also the book which contained all the scientific wisdom of the world, if one only knew how to read it and to interpret its secrets. The prophets were revered as the inspired commentators on the Torah, and the salvation and judgment which they proclaimed pointed beyond themselves to the present, and final, generation: they were 'written down for our instruction, upon whom the end of the ages has come'.[26] On the one hand the scriptural word interpreted the present,

[25] Acts 9; 22; 26.   [26] Cf. I Cor. 10.11.

linking its situation closely with the God-guided history of former times. But it was also accounted to be a light on the path of the godly, which illuminated his future actions. The men of God in the Bible, with their vicissitudes and their own deeds, were the pattern for those who now knew themselves to be the servants of God.

Moreover, it is necessary to be familiar with Old Testament interpretation at the time of Jesus, for it was this above all which gave the religious groups of late Judaism their particular stamp. The spirit of late Judaism is moulded by its interpretation and moves in a different orbit from the logic of modern scholarship. Because the Jewish thinker had learnt to see the highly varied testimonies contained in the Scriptures as the single organic whole of the Word of God, he was in a position to find connections where we only see crass contrasts. Unlike the modern scholar, who probes and analyses with a view to tracing the tiniest originally autonomous units within the books of the Bible, the Jewish scribe tied together with the threads of speculative piety even what seems to us to be irreconcilable. He rejoiced over every little exegetical discovery achieved by combination, exulting in his ever-widening insight into the mystery of revelation which, like God himself, must in the last resort be one.

Most impressive – if only because of its magnitude – is the exegetical work of the rabbis as it is found in the Midrashim (commentaries, primarily on the five books of Moses) and in the collections of laws in the Mishnah, Tosefta and the two Talmuds. Familiarity with these immense and difficult writings is becoming increasingly obligatory for New Testament scholars and teachers.[27] Of course, the larger part of this rabbinic material derives from a later period (the second to the fifth century AD). What the Sadducees and

[27] A good introduction is H. L. Strack, *Introduction to the Talmud and Midrash*, New York–Philadelphia 1959.

Pharisees at the time of Jesus believed and taught cannot be deduced out of hand from the rabbinic writings. The fall of Jerusalem meant a break in the tradition, hope of the coming of the Messiah and the Last Judgment in particular being much diminished.

Where expectation of the great turning point and the triumph of truth and justice seems to have remained unsubdued was in what are called the apocalyptic writings. From these records of mysterious revelations a speculative piety speaks to us about the end of history. The most important of them are the Book of Jubilees, Ethiopian Enoch and II Esdras, sometimes known as the Ezra Apocalypse.[28] The same hope is incandescent in the compilers of the Dead Sea Scrolls. These writings, which were discovered in caves near the Dead Sea in the years following the second world war, will be frequently mentioned below.[29] Their value for an understanding of the New Testament and the activity of Jesus cannot be overestimated, although they have no specifically Christian content – that is, there is no recognition of Jesus as Messiah. Indeed, not so much as the name of Jesus is mentioned – hardly unexpectedly, since these writings date from before the time of Jesus. None the less, they are of the highest importance. They derive from the monastic community of Qumran – the name given today to the ruins on the west coast of the Dead Sea which two thousand years ago housed a Jewish monastery. With this monastic community we suddenly have before our eyes the picture of a group which was still living not far from Jerusalem at the time of Jesus and which was filled with expectations similar

[28] The best edition of these writings is R. H. Charles, *Apocrypha and Pseudepigrapha of the Old Testament*, Oxford 1913 (1963).

[29] Good and complete translations can be found in A. Dupont-Sommer, *The Essene Writings from Qumran*, Oxford 1961, and G. Vermes, *The Dead Sea Scrolls in English*, Penguin Books 1962. The nomenclature adopted here for individual documents is that given by Vermes.

to those of Jesus and his disciples. Much Gospel material now appears in a new light.

The Dead Sea writings also have a methodological interest. The men of Qumran who speak to us in them must be identified with the Essenes, a Jewish sect which was described by the philosopher Philo (a contemporary of Jesus) and by the slightly later historian Josephus.[30] Both Philo and Josephus write from the point of view of outsiders; they were not members of the community. Yet they were not neutral and detached either, but were filled with pride in their virtuous fellow-countrymen. Philo sets up the Essenes as a shining example to his Greek-educated readers. He was convinced that the goal of a truly free existence – the aim of contemporary philosophy – had been reached by this Essene community, with its commitment to the Old Testament fathers. Philo thus presented his account as a kind of *kerygma* which pleaded for existential implementation. Yet the personal testimony of the Essenes as it has come to light in the Dead Sea Scrolls shows that Philo's *kerygma* rests on historically accurate facts. Often the facts are stylistically differentiated from the philosopher's expository additions. Josephus interpreted less and allowed more room for the historical facts. But even where he deliberately compares Essene eschatology with Greek teaching on the fate of the soul after death, he is not inventing but maintains a firm foundation of fact. It is in general remarkable how admirably the personal testimony of the Essenes contained in the Dead Sea Scrolls is supplemented by the accounts of two outside observers: without their contribution our picture of the monastic community in Qumran would be far more colourless and perhaps even incorrect.

[30] These descriptions are contained in Dupont-Sommer's edition. A convenient translation of the *De Bello Judaico* is Flavius Josephus, *The Great Roman-Jewish War*, Harper Torchbooks 1960.

A similar comparison is possible on the basis of the recently discovered Coptic-gnostic documents of Nag-Hammadi in Upper Egypt. Christian gnosticism was hitherto known to us primarily through the accounts of the early Fathers, such as Irenaeus, Tertullian, Hippolytus and Epiphanius. They were all bitter opponents of the gnostic heresy and have therefore always been open to the suspicion of having painted a distorted picture of gnosticism, marked by a deliberate unwillingness to understand it. But in spite of all their polemic, the Fathers were not far astray in their characterization of the various gnostic tendencies. The original Greek form of one of the Nag-Hammadi writings, the *Apocryphon of John*, was used as a source by Irenaeus in the composition of one of the sections of his book *Against the Heresies*.[31]

Both *kerygma* and polemic, then, make use of historical facts and can stand up to questioning on them. Our knowledge of the historical Jesus is also based on facts like these; it is they which permit a representation of his words and work. The leading German New Testament scholars today have turned their attention with great energy to hermeneutics, the art of interpretation, concentrating on the problem of how the message of the Bible must be proclaimed to modern man as the Word of God. There is no doubt that the diminishing interest in the church is due in no small part to the fact that its preaching is viewed as irrelevant, and it is therefore important to introduce the Scriptures in such a way that they make a decisive impact on the life and thought of the hearer. Yet the question of what really happened must not be ignored; the historical facts are important, even in the interests of the *kerygma*.

[31] I.29. See W. Till, *Die gnostischen Schriften des koptischen Papyrus Berolinensis 8502*, Texte und Untersuchungen 60 (V. 2), Berlin 1955, p. 33.

2

WHAT WE KNOW ABOUT THE ACTIVITY OF JESUS

(a) The Background: John the Baptist and the Desert Community at Qumran

IT IS certain that Jesus was baptized by John the Baptist and that he continued John's preaching (Mark 1.9, 14, 15). This means, however, that his activity stood under the shadow of eschatological expectation,[1] as did the activity of John the Baptist and the life of the desert community at Qumran.

The certainty of these groups that God's coming to judgment and the day of salvation was imminent was derived from prophecies, especially the last chapters of the books of Ezekiel and Daniel. It was a conviction that let loose power capable of transforming a whole way of life. In Qumran it took the form of a penitential attitude, repentance in the face of the divine encounter. Each individual tried to win the approval of God and was convinced that this was only possible in the community of saints, the elect of God. Only the saint, the man angelically pure of heart and body, can abide the presence of God – that was the principle which moulded the eschatological expectation of the Essenes; but its practical application was drawn from the Old Testa-

[1] See E. Käsemann, 'Zum Thema der urchristlichen Apokalyptik', *Exegetische Versuche und Besinnungen* II, Göttingen 1964, pp. 105-30 (English translation in preparation).

ment. The men of Qumran derived the basic rules for their much admired monastically ascetic *vita communis* from the directions for the priests who served before the holy majesty of God in the temple and from the instructions given to the armies of Israel in the Holy War. That was the origin of the bodily washings and the rejection of marriage, the shared property and shared labour, and the common meal.[2] What applied to the priests in the Old Testament was now in Qumran extended to the laity. This exegetical step was largely determined by the account of God's appearance on Sinai. When God made a covenant with Israel and gave it the Law, he commanded the people to prepare themselves by washing their clothes and by three days' abstention from sexual intercourse (Ex. 19.10-11, 14-15). Because, however, the precise date of God's coming was concealed from the men in Qumran and every moment in this world might be the last, they had to stand in constant readiness. This holy service, which in the Old Testament is only prescribed for certain people and then only for a short time, could, under the shadow of eschatological expectation, no longer be broken off; thus a sanctification limited in time became a monastic existence cut off from the world.

The description of God's coming on Sinai and the making of the covenant was taken as an indication of what was to happen at the end of time: as before, God will descend, accompanied by lightning and thunder, and will burn up all impurity in the fire of his glory; with the godly elect, however, he will renew the covenant, joining them together with the angels in an eternal communion of saints. Only then will Israel have reached its goal and have fulfilled the conditions

[2] I have shown how this took place in detail in 'Le ministère cultuel dans la secte de Qûmran et dans le Christianisme primitif', *Recherches Bibliques* IV, 1959, 163-202. For the whole question of Essene exegesis see my books *Offenbarung und Schriftforschung in der Qumransekte*, Tübingen 1960, and *Der Paraklet*, Leiden 1963.

which were once laid down on Sinai, and which since that time have illuminated its progress through history: to be a kingdom of priests and a holy nation (Ex. 19.6).

Because God had revealed himself on the remote mountain of Sinai and was miraculously present especially during Israel's wanderings through the wilderness, it was in the desert, near the lonely Dead Sea, that the men of Qumran who waited for God's coming set up their camp. As the Israelites once fled from fertile but godless and now tyrannical Egypt, so the Essenes separated themselves from the populated parts of Israel and went out into the desert; civilization was to them impure and ruled by evil powers. They were strengthened in their resolve by the command of the mysterious voice proclaimed by the prophet: 'In the wilderness prepare the way of the Lord' (Isa. 40.3). They interpreted 'preparing the way' as ceaseless enquiry into the will of God as it was to be found in the scriptures.[3] However, it was accepted in Qumran that all strivings towards godliness remained in the last resort imperfect. For in these last evil days the devil was finally gathering up all his forces to attack the community of the righteous and attempting to shake them by temptations and assaults of every kind. Salvation was therefore the gift of God. At his coming he would cleanse the elect with the Holy Spirit as with purifying waters and would free them from every spirit of error.[4]

The evangelists introduce John the Baptist with the words of Isa. 40.3, which were of such significance for Qumran. They see in him the crier whose voice is heard in the wilderness, calling them to prepare the way for the coming of God (Mark 1.2-4 and parallels) – indeed the man who in the spirit and power of Elijah is to create a people prepared for the Lord (Luke 1.16-17). John preached repentance, i.e. he

[3] Community Rule 8.15-16.   [4] Community Rule 4.20-22.

summoned his hearers to give the aspirations of their hearts a new direction and to see life in the light of the judgment that was soon to break in upon it. The penitent were baptized by him in the River Jordan and understood this immersion as the outward sign both of their change of heart and of the divinely conferred forgiveness of sins.

John was greater than any one of the men of Qumran, near as he stood to them physically and spiritually. True, like them he lived in the desert, ate locusts and wild honey, and clothed himself in a garment of camel hair, as was usual among desert nomads (Mark 1.6 par.). Qumran makes the reason for this ascetic way of life clear. As the son of a priest, John – like the priest-led Essenes – was concerned with the levitical purity of his person. In order to keep himself pure and unspotted from the world, he had to be economically independent. But his call to repentance was addressed to the world; it was addressed to the men who in Qumran had, practically speaking, been 'written off'. John showed that the God of grace was also to be found outside the church, the institution of salvation. He offered everyone the possibility of repentance and flight from the wrathful judgment of God that was to come (Luke 3.7-8). Nor did John hold his penitents to a monastically ascetic life in the desert; he sent them back to their former callings and stations in life (Luke 3.10-14); it was presumably only a small group of disciples who stayed outside in the desert with him. The place of the daily bathings practised in Qumran was taken by the single immersion which, as in Qumran, pointed towards the baptism with the Holy Spirit as the eschatological and complete act of purification (Mark 1.8). This method of baptism was the reason why John was called 'the Baptist'.

Jesus took the step that even John did not dare to take. He worked in the world; for him the desert was only an occasional refuge. The evangelists tell how after John's arrest Jesus went to Galilee and began to preach openly, 'Repent, for the time is fulfilled and the kingdom of God is at hand' (Mark 1.15 par.). In the view of the people Galilee was hardly a possible home or place of activity for a great man;[5] it counted as Galilee of the Gentiles, the country of those who dwelt in the shadow of death (Matt. 4.15-16). Yet Jesus went there, not flinching even from the darkest places of Jewish life but opening the door of repentance and new life to the despised tax-collectors and prostitutes. These people were not only separated from devout and respected citizens by the barriers of decency and morality; more, by consorting with them the righteous man was risking his purity, his right to belong to the community of saints and godly men. In Qumran it was only after a trial period of three years that a postulant was accepted into full member-ship and admitted to the sacred meal; up to then he still counted as impure. Jesus, however, ate with the publicans and called one of them away from tax-collecting to become one of his disciples (Matt. 9.9-10). This unusual association with sinners, so shocking to the devout Jew, must be ac-counted an especially characteristic mark of the historical Jesus. And it was precisely this behaviour which almost in-evitably brought Jesus into conflict with the regulations about outward purity which were so scrupulously observed by Pharisees and Essenes alike (Mark 7.1-23 par.). Nor did Jesus baptize. There was nothing of the ascetic about him; in contrast to John the Baptist, he was called a glutton and a wine-bibber (Matt. 11.18-19). Finally, he set himself, pro-vocatively and in sovereign manner, above the laws of sab-bath observance wherever they interfered with his actions. That, too, is certainly historical. For the Palestinian Chris-tians kept the sabbath in the Jewish way; they had therefore

[5] Cf. John 1.46; 7.52.

no reason to make up stories in which Jesus broke the regulations about the day of rest.[6]

Thus it was the earthly Jesus who already displayed the power which broke the fetters of the ceremonially-bound thinking of a cult tied to holy places and occasions – the power which later made possible missions and the mass conversion of the heathen. These world-wide consequences of Jesus' actions were better understood by Paul than by the disciples who followed Jesus during his lifetime.

(b) Jesus' Message about the Coming of the Kingdom of God

(i) The call to repentance as good news

The coming of the kingdom of God, paraphrased by Matthew as 'the kingdom of heaven', was the primary theme of Jesus' message. With this he proclaimed that God would presently establish his kingly rule on earth once and for all, and would make an end of sin and all evil. The breaking in of the 'rule of God' – that is what is meant by the Hebrew or Aramaic expression used – marks a complete turning point; for God's actions and his rule are in stark contrast to the works of man.

In the faith of Israel the kingly rule of God already holds a central place. It is celebrated particularly in the Psalms;[7] God's rule means security against the forces of chaos, which threaten the stability of the world, and victory over Israel's enemies. It is everlasting, yet must be enforced again and again and be manifested anew to all men. The kingly rule of God also appears in the late Jewish apocalyptic writ-

---

[6] See W. Rordorf, *Sunday*, London and Philadelphia 1968, pp. 54 ff.

[7] God's kingly rule is mentioned explicitly in Psalm 103.19; 145.11-13; the 'enthronement psalms' should also, however, be included here.

ings,[8] as the eschatological event, the final end of the tyrannical kingdoms of the world. All in all, however, the concept of 'the rule of God' is rare, both in the Old Testament and in the apocalyptic writings. It is almost totally absent from the Dead Sea Scrolls;[9] Paul seldom uses it and in rabbinic writings it has lost much of its eschatological gloss. For these reasons alone there can be no doubt that the concept is an intrinsic part of Jesus' message.

In Qumran, when they spoke of the great turning point, it was the judgment, earthquakes and consuming fire that they had in mind, and in looking for the salvation of the godly they thought of their own community. The community of the righteous formed the bridge between the darkness of the present and the glorious era of God; it was therefore the primary object of faith. Jesus, on the other hand, and perhaps already John the Baptist, talked about the rule of God: since God is to bring about the great turning point, when it will happen and what the new era will look like is in his hand alone.

The doctrines of Qumran and the call of John the Baptist had the power of fear; they threatened people with the coming judgment and the consuming outbreak of the divine wrath; the only remaining chance of enduring this judgment

---

[8] Cf. Tobit 13.1; Enoch 22.14; 25.3; 27.3; 84.2; 103.1 (God's constant dominion). God's rule is eschatological in *Assumptio Mosis* 10.1; *Oracula Sibyllina* 3.767, and rule is given by God according to Daniel 2.44; 7.14, 18, 22, 27.

[9] God's kingly rule is mentioned in the War Rule (6.6; 12.7); according to 6.6 it will come into effect when victory has been achieved in the war of the end-time. In the Blessings (1QS b 4. 26), the kingdom of the end-time is to be understood in spatial terms. The term 'kingdom (kingly rule) of God' (*malkuth-shamayim*) does not, however, occur in any of these passages. It is important that the commentary on the prophecy of Nathan, understood in a messianic way, inserts a quotation from Ex. 15.17-18: 'The place, O Lord, which thy hands have established. The Lord will reign for ever and ever.' The sanctuary founded by God is the community of the end-time, the most important feature in the time of God's kingly rule.

was complete repentance. Such preaching demanded a decision from its hearers; it had a 'critical' power. Qumran's teacher met with only scorn and derision from many; but he knew that he had been appointed as a trap for scorners and transgressors, as their doom in the divine judgment. To the simple, however, who allowed their hearts to be touched, he proclaimed the good tidings of God's mercy and forgiveness.[10] Everything depended on repentance, the turning away from the old life; the confession of sins played an important part (*Community Rule* 1.22-24). Viewed positively, repentance was a turning to the Mosaic Law as interpreted by the community and as realized in the communion of the elect; it was a question of accepting and performing 'the truth', the radically interpreted will of God. The penitential mood thus led to the decision to apply for admission to the Qumran community, because only there could the true fruits of repentance be brought forth (*Community Rule* 5.1-11). The rabbis also stressed repentance; it was one of the seven things that proceeded from the counsel of God before the creation of the world.[11]

Jesus, too, preached repentance. He branded pride and hardness of heart as the gravest sins (Matt. 12.39-42) and assured the man with the broken and contrite heart of God's forgiving goodness (Luke 18.9-14). In so doing he continued the preaching of John the Baptist and the Teacher of Righteousness. But what was the new element in Jesus' preaching? What unique and incomparable element is there in the testimony of the Gospels and in our own confession of Jesus? Gerhard Ebeling sees *faith* as the focal point of the activity of Jesus and the significant aspect of his work for us.[12] All the aspects of what we know about Jesus come

[10] Thanksgiving Hymns 2.8-15; 18.12-15.
[11] Pirke Rabbi Eliezer, ch. 3.
[12] 'Jesus and Faith' in: *Word and Faith* (London and Philadelphia 1963), pp. 201-46.

together, he believes, in faith; faith is what 'comes to expression' in the work and words of Jesus; it claims us and addresses us. This does not happen so much through Jesus speaking of his faith or demonstrating it as an attitude to be imitated, but rather through the promise of faith which he kindles and confirms in those who have no hope, and through the witness of faith which he shows by his life for others to be the reality by which he is supported. Just as Paul and Luther saw in God's righteousness not so much a property which is confined to God as a power through which he purposes to make men righteous, so Ebeling sees in the faith of Jesus something active and creative: Jesus radiated faith, and gave it to others. Ebeling makes this clear by means of the Gospel evidence. For example, Jesus did not wait for his word of power to be confirmed in faith in the other man's response of 'Amen', as was the custom in Judaism. He himself spoke the 'Amen' and used it to preface his declared intentions. In this way both word and hearer were brought within the sphere of God's power, in which the word is demonstrated to be truth and the hearer is brought to believe in this truth.[13] Jesus 'pro-voked' faith, called it forth, in both senses of the word: he aroused it and discovered it in those who appealed to him for healing: he called it to light by confirming it as the power of deliverance for the helpless: 'Great is your faith!' 'May it be to you as you have believed!' 'Your faith has saved you!' (Mark 5.34; 9.23-24; 10.52; Matt. 8.10, 13; 9.28-29; 15.28; Luke 17.19.)

Ebeling's existential interpretation of the historical Jesus is very impressive. It also takes us quickly beyond the historical Jesus: the category of faith provides a good bridge to the Christ of the *kerygma*. For the *kerygma*, too, demands faith, and in both cases it is concerned with Jesus: the his-

[13] Op. cit., pp. 236 ff.

torical Jesus, who has testified to saving faith for others through his words and actions, is acknowledged by his disciples at Easter as the content of faith and as himself the deliverer. It is, however, striking that the evangelists say virtually nothing about the faith of Jesus: could these first witnesses to Jesus have missed the point of Jesus' witness, which was expressed in what he said? Faith is never related directly to the kingdom of God. Nothing would have been more obvious than to demand faith as an existential answer to this chief theme of Jesus' preaching, faith brought about by God to help to bridge the gulf between what cannot be seen in the present and what is still to come in the future. But Jesus evidently did not do that. Why not? Has Ebeling overestimated the role of faith? Three points would seem to be relevant here.

1.   Ebeling believes that the way in which the concept of faith is oriented towards persons, as is clear from the words to the healed man which have just been quoted, is a striking peculiarity; he knows no parallel to it from late Judaism.[14] But this form of expression was already to be found in Qumran. The interpreters of Qumran saw the famous verse 'The righteous shall live by his faithfulness (or: his faith)' (Hab. 2.4) fulfilled among the members of their own community and in the end-time. They were the righteous, because they had proved themselves by keeping the Law, and they would live for ever 'because of their labours and because of their faith in the Teacher of Righteousness' (*Habakkuk Commentary* 8.1-3). Here, too, faith[15] is thought of in personal terms and associated with the personal pronoun;[16]

[14] Op. cit., p. 238.
[15] That faith and not trust is mentioned here arises from an earlier passage in the Habakkuk Commentary. In 2.6-8 it is said of the enemies of the Qumran community that 'they did not believe' when they heard from the mouth of the Teacher what would dawn on the last generation.
[16] This is also required by the Old Testament model.

and as in the declaration of Jesus, 'Your faith has saved you',
it has saving power. Faith in the Teacher of Righteousness
was demanded by his message that the end was near at
hand and that therefore it was necessary to repent (2.6-8).
Jesus, too, proclaimed apocalyptic tidings of this kind, and
the full significance of his promise becomes clear against the
background of our parallels from Qumran. Faith has
brought deliverance not only from sickness but also from
eternal damnation; it has led to the salvation brought about
by the rule of God.[17] In the Qumran text, however, faith
does not stand alone, but is accompanied by concern over
the Law: the penitent of Qumran returns to the Torah. In
the sayings of Jesus the temporal aspect is also different:
Jesus announces that deliverance – eschatological deliverance! – has already been achieved, whereas at Qumran it is
promised as a future reward.

The rabbis, too, recognized the saving power of faith. In
the Mekilta, a commentary on the book of Exodus, there is
a theological discussion of the deliverance of the Israelites
at the Reed Sea. In the foreground stands the question, Why
did Israel deserve this miracle? What moved God to inter-
vene and save them? Among other reasons, faith is mentioned. One of the rabbis makes God say to Israel at the
Reed Sea: 'The faith with which your father Abraham believed in me merits my dividing the sea for you.' Another
points to the faith of Israel, using the same expression.[18]
But even here, faith is not used absolutely and does not
appear as the only possible and appropriate relationship of
man to God.

[17] It is also clear that the admonition 'Believe in the Gospel'
(Mark 1.12) which accompanies Jesus' call to repentance rightly
expresses what that call demands.
[18] *Mekilta, Tractate Beshallaḥ*, Wayyehi 6 on Ex. 14.22. According to J. Bär (*Israel Be'Ammim*, Jerusalem 1955, p. 127, n. 3) such
testimonies of faith were also known in Israel before Paul.

2.   The central significance of faith emerges in the apocalyptic writings. For them, Israel's deliverance at the Reed Sea is a great example of God's saving action to strengthen faith at the end-time (*War Rule* 11.9-10), and Paul elucidates the nature of eschatological existence by means of Abraham's faith. In his attempt to demonstrate the nature of faith by means of the historical Jesus, Ebeling has overlooked the historically conditioned, apocalyptic element and has thus altered his quest for the concept of faith by means of a phenomenological approach. We certainly know that the historical Jesus proclaimed the coming of the kingdom of God and preached repentance; his whole work is eschatologically determined. In Ebeling's account, however, faith is divorced from its connection with the kingdom of God and apocalyptic;[19] this can be seen from the very fact that concepts like 'the rule of God' and 'repentance' are missing. But the very fact that the end was thought to be imminent explains why Jesus demands faith only rarely: because of the coming rule of God he *preached repentance*, proclaimed faith as *being penitent*. Had Jesus only spoken of faith, it is difficult to see why he should have died on the cross.

It is the call to repentance that opens up a gulf between the preacher and his audience; the Old Testament prophets and John the Baptist had experienced this in their own persons. The preacher of repentance becomes a stumbling block; he frightens those who think they are righteous from the cover of their self-certainty and arouses the sinners from their lethargy. He demands faith, but it is faith as conversion, re-appraisal and a new self-understanding. He requires the pious man to burn what he has worshipped and acknowledge that he is a sinner, and he gives the sinner

---

[19] This is true even where Ebeling defines faith as being by nature related to the future (pp. 240 f.).

courage to do what he had regarded as impossible, to repent and believe in God's forgiveness. Only the call to penitence makes it clear what faith means, that God is all that matters and that he demands the whole man. It seems to me that Jesus' call to repentance has lost none of its urgency today. It is precisely the autonomous man, the modern man, who must learn that there is no way to faith except through repentance and that only the man who has lost faith in the continuance of the world without God and his own power to do good can find a ground for his existence in God. God is there for the desperate man, for the man who needs him; there is no point in offering faith to the man who is not ready to repent.

3. The stumbling block which must be overcome by eschatological faith is therefore not the message, but the messenger. Ebeling has shown that even in the Old Testament, faith in God's Word includes trust in his person. This is true even more of the prophet of the end-time. How does he know that the day of the Lord is at hand and that this day will be darkness and not light? What is the basis of his claim to be God's ambassador in the hour of decision? Furthermore, Jesus went far beyond the preachers of his time both in word and action. He performed his healing miracles as a sign that the reign of God had already dawned, that here the power of God was at work. Therefore in the Gospels, too, faith is directed towards the action of Jesus and is mentioned in connection with his miracles of healing. The believer who cries out to God for deliverance is directed to Jesus, because in him alone is the power of the approaching God effective. At this point it becomes clear that the faith appropriate to the historical Jesus is the faith in Christ demanded by the *kerygma*: in both cases Jesus is seen as God's eschatological instrument on earth.

Jesus is also unique in proclaiming repentance as good

tidings; according to Mark he preached 'the Gospel of God' as he trod in the footsteps of John the Baptist (1.14). 'Gospel' means an invitation to all to accept God's forgiveness and to live from it. Whereas in Qumran the two camps of the repentant and the hard-hearted were thought of with blessings and curses respectively (*Community Rule* 2.1-10), Jesus (in the beatitudes) proclaimed blessedness and woe (Luke 6.20-26). That is to say, he proclaimed the norm of divine judgment but did not himself judge, delivering no one over to the punitive wrath of God. The present was for him a time of patience;[20] where the Gospels speak of a punitive divine intervention in this age and give details of the last judgment it is the Christian community that is speaking.[21] In Qumran they taught that all the elect must be loved, while those rejected by God were to be hated (*Community Rule* 1.3-4); but Jesus forbade hate in general, even hate of an enemy, demanding intercessory prayer instead of curses (Matt. 5.44). In Qumran the elect and the righteous were gathered together; Jesus, on the other hand, came as physician to the sick and saviour of sinners. He saw the movement of repentance not, as they did in Qumran, as reversion to a radically interpreted Law but as a return to the open arms of the Father. God had more pleasure in the homecoming of a single sinner than over the faithfulness of many righteous (Luke 15). The fact that Jesus confronted men with God and forced them to decision cannot, as we have seen, be counted as at all unique, since this is also true of the preaching of John the Baptist and the men of Qumran. What is new is that the decision for the rule of God is a glad one: Jesus compares it with the behaviour of a labourer who finds a treasure in a field and sells all that he

[20] See the parables of the wheat and the tares and the net (Matt. 13.24-30, 47-50), and the barren fig tree (Luke 13.6-9).
[21] See my article 'The Dichotomized Servant and the End of Judas Iscariot', *Revue de Qûmran* 6 (1964), pp. 43-58.

has in order to possess it, or with the joy of a merchant who willingly gives all his worldly goods in return for a splendid pearl (Matt. 13.44-46).

It is also astounding that Jesus rejected the judgment of his pious contemporaries and even stood it on its head: anyone who despairs of himself because he is despised by the world, and even feels that he is lost as far as the final judgment is concerned, will find comfort and deliverance if he seeks God with an upright heart. It is true that in Qumran, too, the only way to God's righteousness is through repentance and the sorrowful recognition that man is guilty and has strayed far from the right path (*Damascus Rule* 1.8-10). There, too, only the man who renounces his own righteousness and makes himself humble before God is truly righteous (*Thanksgiving Hymns* 4.30-40). But in Qumran considerable importance was attached to the fruits of repentance, and therefore penitence led to a pious mode of life and justification by grace to a striving for holiness. Jesus, on the other hand, wills man to put his whole trust in God, in the father who does not reject his child, in the redeemer who breaks the chain of sin and in the creator who makes men new.

Jesus also demanded complete conversion and the unconditional fulfilment of the will of God; and he, too, found this will expressed in the law of the Old Testament (Matt. 5.17-42). But he wanted all action to spring from love of God. The Hebrew-Aramaic word used by Jesus for the 'will' of God really means his 'pleasure' – only the spontaneous action springing from love can truly 'give pleasure'. Jesus teaches in the spirit of Deuteronomy, which also set its stamp on Qumran piety. This book interprets all individual laws as the unfolding of the great commandment, pronounced thrice daily in prayer, to love and serve God alone (6.4-5); it sees in such love the answer to the love of

God towards Israel.[22] In Qumran, God was spoken of as Father and his love was compared with the devoted care of a nurse towards her baby (*Thanksgiving Hymns* 9.34-35). But basically it was only the 'son of his truth', i.e., the elect and member of the community, who could confidently rely on God's fatherly goodness. Jesus demanded of everyone that they should meet God like a child who on his own initiative acquires the characteristics of his father and wishes to please him in everything (Matt. 5.48). But he sets the indicative, what God is, before the imperative, what he commands: because we are all God's children and only exist by virtue of his fatherly goodness, we should live before him as real children and be perfect like the heavenly Father (Matt. 5.44-48).

With the demand that everyone should live in a state of complete, childlike love towards the heavenly Father, Jesus assumed a state of affairs which, according to the apocalyptic view, can only be realized in the last days. In the day of the Lord, when the rule of God is all in all, the state of being the child of God will also be truly possible: the Israelites will then become children of the living God, receiving his Spirit and fulfilling his commandments (*Book of Jubilees* 1.23-25). In accord with the Old Testament, the rabbis called Israel the son of God. Nevertheless, they could also say that God did not deliver the seed of Abraham from Egypt in order to make him his child but in order to keep him as his servant. For when he gave the Israelites the commandments and they were unwilling to accept them, he was in a position to say 'You are my servants'.[23] The image of the servant who obeys the commands of his master without contradiction characterized the relationship to God;

[22] G. von Rad, *Old Testament Theology* I, Edinburgh 1962, p. 230.
[23] Siphre Numeri 15, 41, 115, 35a.

even the idea of God as Father was determined by this picture.

Jesus, on the other hand, proclaimed the liberty of the children of God as if the eschatological hope were already fulfilled. Because the end-time corresponds to the ideal primal time, he turned to the first beginnings, to the creation and its perfect order, so well-pleasing to God. From this he derived the norm of human action and therefore ruthlessly by-passed the Mosaic Law. Jesus saw in certain commandments emergency regulations, as it were, for a fallen and hard-hearted humanity, which had to have concessions made to it (Mark 10.2-9). At the beginning, however, when the first man and woman still lived like good children in the presence of God the Father, this was not necessary; nor will there be any compromise at the end, when God's true will takes effect. This interpretation of the Mosaic Law was also unprecedented. The first Jerusalem Christians did not dare to take any step to supersede the Torah; and for that very reason it is clear that we are here dealing once more with the historical Jesus.

But Jesus did not entirely rescind the Sinaitic Law. He gave it a new interpretation, lending it a new force in the light of the coming of the kingdom of God. Certainly in so doing he passed over the letter in order to go back to the will of God itself. The same thing happened when Jesus, summing up the whole of the Law, set up one, all-inclusive, supreme commandment (Mark 12.29-31). Such a doctrine was not really new. Philo describes the sum total of Essene piety as love towards God and one's neighbour,[24] and Hippolytus says similarly of the Essenes that on entry into the community they took an oath to fear God and act justly towards men.[25] The *Community Rule* sees in the seeking

[24] *Quod omnis probus liber sit*, 83-84.
[25] *Refutatio Haeresium* IX, 23.

after God's will the essence of true existence (1.2). But since Qumran found the will of God in the commandments, in the last resort the attempt to pass beyond concrete demands to the heart of God itself failed. The synthesis of the will of God into a simple basic law crumbled, constantly disintegrating into a multitude of individual commandments.

Jesus regarded the twofold commandment of love towards God and one's neighbour as the summing up of the Law. Only where we meet everyone, even an enemy, with unqualified love are we acting in the sphere of the perfection recognized before God, are we within the domain of the love of God (Matt. 5.43-48).

Like these two commandments, eschatological expectation and the demand for obedience form a strict unity in Jesus' preaching which must be preserved. Liberal exegesis inclines to overlook the apocalyptic components which point towards the future, or to push them aside as a mythically-coloured notion conditioned by the age; according to this view only the faith-founded ethic, the demand for righteousness and love of one's neighbour, as these are expressed in the parables, for instance, or in the Sermon on the Mount, have permanent value. In *Jesus and the Word*, Bultmann ruthlessly exposes the faults of liberal exegesis, showing how it read its own ideals into Jesus' message. But Bultmann and his followers do not entirely escape the danger of a stunted interpretation of Jesus' preaching either; only it is now Heidegger instead of Kant who offers the exegetical key. Bultmann, for example, thinks that the coming of the kingdom is not really an event in time and that the kingdom of God is not an entity which begins in the present and is perfected in the future; it has neither a 'where' nor a 'when'. In this view, the future of which Jesus speaks is whatever comes to meet man, whatever forces him to decision; and every hour when man is confronted with decision is the

hour of judgment. According to Bultmann the whole of contemporary mythology was, with Jesus, at the service of
human existence; in the light of this he saw his hour as the
hour of judgment and proclaimed it as such.[26] The result of
this interpretation is similar to that of liberal theology, except that in the place of ethical demands we now have the
call to decision and the realization of true existence. The
temporal line shrinks to the pin-point of here and now; and
the call to decision is qualified and radicalized by eschatological expectation. Käsemann is able to say that Jesus
meant that 'with his word the *basileia* comes to his hearers'
and Fuchs agrees with this view.[27] As we shall see later, with
the acts of Jesus the rule of God does reach into the present
and give it new content. Yet his expectation remains directed
towards a real, temporally-conceived future. That fact must
not be glossed over in an existential interpretation of the
concepts 'future' and 'eschatological'.

J. M. Robinson takes a course similar to Bultmann's, tele-
scoping dialectically the apocalyptic succession of present
and future. Looking at the beatitudes, he finds that in
poverty the rule of God is to be found, in hunger plenitude,
in tears joy, etc.[28] In this way the future in the second part of
the proclamation is reinterpreted into a present and the
sharp contrast between 'now' and 'then' is blurred by a
curious paradox which would hardly have satisfied the
original hearers. In fact Jesus had no such intention. True,
with his activity the kingdom of God has begun, but it is not
yet revealed in all its power; the full realization of the salvation which ends all tribulation is still reserved for the future.
As with the liberals, there is here embarrassment in the face

[26] R. Bultmann, *Jesus and the Word*, p. 47.
[27] 'Jesus' Understanding of Time', *Studies of the Historical Jesus*,
London 1964, p. 106, n. 1.
[28] J. M. Robinson, 'The Formal Structure of Jesus' Message',
p. 103.

of the alien, all too Jewish Jesus. Thanks to the investigations of the 'history of religions' school, Bultmann and his followers know more about the apocalyptic writings than was possible in the nineteenth century. The rule of God is not just the embodiment of a new morality or an ethical ideal. Jesus' expectation of the end of the world was, according to Bultmann, mythology, just like the notion of demons and of Satan as the great opponent of God.

It is understandable that in preaching to people of the present day these ideas are freshly interpreted and presented non-mythologically. But this must not lead us to think that the Jesus of history really thought non-mythologically too, seeing only what the rule of God meant for his own day and believing only in the evil purposes of men, not in the devil.[29] Nor did apocalyptic interpretations flower for the first time under the primitive church. For Jesus himself already thought apocalyptically. One of the few sayings of Jesus to which Paul refers deals with the order of the resurrection (I Thess. 4.15) and hence with a particular apocalyptic problem. And the saying that the coming of the kingdom will be experienced by the present generation (Mark 9.1) presupposes that Jesus had an apocalyptic calendar; I am thinking of the obscure prophecy in Daniel 9.24-27,[30] which played an important part in the Judaism of the time.

Even Jesus' words about trusting in God's goodness are, when all is said and done, eschatologically orientated. Only the man who knows he is the child of God and thus takes up his eschatological position can really say that this world, in spite of all its evil, belongs to the Father. And only the man who has learnt from an apocalyptic standpoint to see the

[29] For Jesus, the notion of Satan in fact has little significance, as in his view the world can only be called evil in so far as men are evil (see Bultmann, *Jesus and the Word*, p. 47).

[30] Cf. also my article 'Der Katechon' in *New Testament Studies* 9 (1963), pp. 276-91.

beauty of creation's beginnings really knows what it is that makes anxious care unnecessary. For it was in paradise that God took from men all anxiety about food and himself dressed them in coats made of animal skins (Gen. 2.16; 3.21). Without the eschatological perspective, Jesus' words about anxiety remain baseless enthusiasm; and it is surely more than chance when Matthew in the middle of them inserts the command 'Seek first the kingdom of God and his righteousness, and all these things shall be yours as well' (6.33).

(ii) *The parables*

In Jesus' preaching of the coming of the kingdom of God, the parable has a firm place as narrative form. No one doubts that most of the parables as they are presented in the Synoptic Gospels are genuine, and in the 'new quest' Jesus the parable-teller receives special attention. The uniqueness of the parable preaching of Jesus is particularly noticeable when it is compared with the Dead Sea Scrolls and the rabbinic parables.

In the Dead Sea writings the end of the world is depicted as a great turning point at which the present order and all its standards will be turned upside down. For the form of this world is anti-God: the devil is in command and the mass of mankind is knowingly or unknowingly subject to him. The righteous man suffers. Only the consciousness that everything will soon be radically different makes it possible for him to bear injustice and oppression. More, his lot fills him with joy and pride. The man who suffers now will soon triumph; he whose worldly fate seems without hope will participate as accuser and avenger at the last judgment.

But these factual statements are clothed in mystery. They are described in terms of the images and prophecies of the Old Testament, there frequently applied to the Israel of the future or to the New Jerusalem, and now related to the community of the saved in the last days. There is a great contrast between the important role which is the lot of the company of the righteous in the divine future and its present small stature. The Qumran writings illustrate and, through hope, overcome this contrast in the same way as Jesus does in the parables of the sower, the seed growing by itself, the grain of mustard seed and the leaven: the inconspicuous beginning is contrasted with the mighty result. The Qumran community is like a plantation in an arid land. It is still small and hidden among high trees. But it cannot wither and sends up a shoot from which grows the eternal, true plantation of the last days. Its root is strong, reaching down to a living and holy spring of water and bringing the plant strength and sap. It does not matter if the passers-by trample on the stem, or if wild beasts feed on its shoots, or if birds nest in the branches. For though unperceived it will endure for ever. God himself protects it through his holy angels and with the fiery flame – like the entrance to paradise. For this plant is paradisal. One day its shadow will fall over the whole world, its branches will reach to the clouds, its roots will drink of the waters from the depths and its boughs will be fed by the rivers of paradise. But the high trees which grow so quickly round about are all doomed to decline, for they do not drink from the well of life and bear no fruit. Yet, it is expressly emphasized, no one guesses these things, no one knows the secret of the plant destined for the end of the world. The worldly man outside has eyes that do not see, and with all his scheming and planning he does not arrive at faith in the living spring (*Thanksgiving Hymns* 8.4-14; 6.15-16).

Two things are clear – the resemblance between this description and the parables of Jesus, and its difference. The image in the *Thanksgiving Hymns* is an extensive one, an allegory whose every detail describes in veiled terms the desert community's interpretation of itself and of its relationship to the world. Even the plantation of trees, so laboriously set near the desert monastery, evidently plays its part. It is not the kingdom of God, with its incomprehensible strangeness, but the community of the saved in its established form, pre-moulded for eternity, which forms the substance of the eschatological hope.

Jesus spoke about the coming rule of God in terse, simple parables. But here and there there are features of the portrayal which are common to both. Jesus, too, used images about sowing, about the tree and the garden, as well as about fields and vineyards – these last significantly absent from the Qumran accounts. He too talked about firm roots and about the plant which shoots up quickly only to wither; he spoke of the seed that falls on the footpath beside the field and is trodden down,[31] and of fruitful and unfruitful trees. He too uses, quite as a matter of course, the emblem of the cosmic tree, which shelters all the birds of the air, to describe the holy, eternal power of the end-time – an image which is applied in the Old Testament to the foreign rulers doomed to destruction (Mark 4.32; cf. Ezek. 31; Dan. 4). Above all, in both places we meet the mystery which surrounds the eschatological order and the true essence of its unity. The outsider perpetually looks on but still without perceiving – this sentence, derived from Isa. 6.9, is quoted not only by Mark (4.12) but already by the Qumran community (*Thanksgiving Hymns* 8.13-14). The mystery of the kingdom can therefore hardly be a later, elaborated theory;

---

[31] It is remarkable how in the allegorical interpretation of the parable of the sower (Mark 4.14-20 par.) the picture of men as God's planting is overlaid by that of the seed and the word of God (see Joachim Jeremias, *The Parables of Jesus*, London 1963, p. 79); we may perhaps detect the influence of Qumran here. The allegorical interpretation has been added by the church.

it must already have had its established place in the preaching of the historical Jesus.

It is worth noting that Jesus confronts the individual with the approaching divine rule. In the Dead Sea writings it is only the leader and founder, the Teacher of Righteousness, who appears as individual actor. He tells no parables; where he speaks metaphorically of himself he associates himself with his followers and the community of which he is a part. For example, he introduces a plantation of trees in which he himself is the diligent gardener. By digging and by looking after the irrigation channels he even manages to bring the trees through the burning heat of summer and keeps them from running wild and reverting to nature (*Thanksgiving Hymns* 8.20-26). This description has no dramatic climax; the teacher merely mentions the catastrophic results for the garden which would follow the removal of his care. Jesus in one of his parables shows the owner of a garden talking to the gardener about the fate of a single tree. Attention is directed to this one tree only: why does it bear no fruit? Will it justify its existence if it is allowed one more year, during which the gardener will give it all the care it needs by digging and fertilizing (Luke 13.6-9)? This short parable is full of suspense and every individual hearer feels himself confronted with the decision.

Moreover, the individual of whom Jesus spoke is not isolated in the desert; he is in the midst of the world. His situation and his actions are illuminated through everyday scenes and dramatic stories: here are the sower and the farmer, the gardener and the vineyard-owner; the shepherd and the merchant; the householder, housewife and labourer, the father and his sons; the king and his guests – figures throng the stage of everyday life and are set in the light of the coming rule of God. The Qumran writings have nothing to say about this living kaleidoscope, this wealth of models of eschatological existence; in this respect they again show their remoteness from the world. The individual loses himself in the community and his world is the desert.

A second image which the Qumran community used to describe its eschatological existence is that of the fortified town. God himself sets its foundation on a rock, produces properly proportioned supports and builds up a framework of tested stones; thus he himself sets up the building (*Thanksgiving Hymns* 6.25-27). In this way he fulfils beyond all expectation the prophecy: He will lay in Zion a tested stone, a precious cornerstone (Isa. 28.16). His building is both stronghold and sanctuary and resembles the temple in Jerusalem. But it does not stand on Zion and is not made with hands. For it is the men who belong to the community of the saved who are meant by the tested stones; they are a living building. The holy, valiant building of the community is unconquerable. He who takes refuge behind the walls of this fortification cannot be swallowed up, even by the gates of hell themselves.

Jesus told no parable about the fortress of the rock-like community. But he too was familiar with this image. It can no longer be a matter of dispute that the famous passage in Matt. 16.18 according to which Jesus promised that he would build his church upon Peter, the man of rock, and the gates of hell should not prevail against it, is closely related to the Qumran conception. In both cases the building on the rock represents the community of the saved, and in both places the threatening power of the gates of hell is mentioned. Only the Qumran text and its background in Isa. 28, which it illuminates, make it clear why these two powers are associated. Isaiah spoke of the miserable end of the scornful, who fancied that they had come to terms with the kingdom of death and were thus armed against all eventualities; but only the man who believes in God and the stone laid by him in Zion will not be confounded (28.14-22). In Qumran the future ruin of the worldly-wise was described: like the company of Korah, they will be swallowed up by the gates of the realm of death, which will spring up during the earthquakes of the end-time (*Thanksgiving Hymns* 3.13-18). Only the house of the community built by God on the rock of truth will be saved from this disaster.[32] Later the rabbis extolled the rock of the temple as the stone that sealed up the realm of death; this idea too is based on Isa. 28.

Qumran also throws new light on Jesus' saying – certainly authentic – about the violent who take the kingdom by force (Matt. 11.12; Luke 16.16). The 'violent' who beleaguer and seize the kingdom (Matt. 11.12), forcing their way into it (cf. Luke 16.16), are not, as might be supposed, impetuous forces of the righteous who wish to force on the coming of the rule of God; they are the enemies of the righteous, led by the devil. In Qumran the final judgment can be presented as a great war; all the Gentiles, as well as the ungodly members of Israel, join together in order to overrun the camp of the holy army. But at the last moment God comes to the rescue of his own with a company of angels and destroys the army of his enemies. Belial and his demons who, as it were, produce and direct evil from behind the scenes of the world stage, will also then be rendered harmless. The prologue to this drama is the struggle for the divine truth which is already raging.

The Old Testament prototype for this eschatological drama was in part the vision of the struggle for the mountain of Jerusalem, in front of which the armies of the heathen will be destroyed by God's miraculous power.[33] In part, too,

---

[32] See my article 'Felsenmann und Felsengemeinde', *Zeitschrift für die Neutestamentliche Wissenschaft* 48 (1957), pp. 314-26.
[33] Isa. 29.1-8; 30.27-33; Ezek. 37; 38.

it was the Sinai tradition. On Sinai Moses sanctified the people and, according to God's command, set bounds round the mountain; no one was to break through these bounds in order to touch the mountain or to look at God. They were a defence for the people, for whoever approaches God's holiness will be destroyed by him.[34]

The passage about the stormers of the kingdom in Matt. 11.12; Luke 16.16 must be seen against this background. From the time of John the Baptist onwards 'every man enters violently into the kingdom' (Luke 16.16). The Greek verb used here is also used in Ex. 19.24 for 'breaking in' to the holy ground on Sinai. Matthew speaks of the 'violent' who 'seize' the kingdom, i.e. try to snatch away the men who stand in the territory of the kingdom of God and to make them waver and desert their cause. Probably there is a play of words here: the violent (Hebrew: *'arîṣîm*) become 'robbers' (Hebrew: *parîṣîm*); just as Jesus can say that the house of God in Jerusalem has become a den of robbers (Mark 11.17), so according to the passages in Matthew and Luke the saints of the kingdom, chosen for the living, eschatological sanctuary, are threatened in a similar manner. On the other hand the rule of God comes with violence (Matt. 11.12): just as the God of Sinai 'breaks out' against everything profane which comes too near him (Ex. 19.22), and in the last days his judgment is to condemn all who ignore the restraints of the Torah (*Damascus Rule* 20.25), so now, according to the words of Jesus, the rule of God is breaking in, helping and healing, victorious in the face of all opposition (cf. Matt. 12.28).[35]

The term *basileia* (*malkuth*), which generally means the kingly rule of God, applies in the passage about the storm-

[34] Ex. 19.10-15, 21-25.
[35] See my article, 'The Eschatological Interpretation of the Sinai Tradition in Qumran and in the New Testament', *Revue de Qûmran* 6 (1967), pp. 89-107.

ing of the kingdom to particular groups of men for whom this rule is already present; they do God's will and are chosen for his kingdom. There is, however, a notable contrast to Qumran; Jesus knew no enclosed group of saints, shut off from the world; the company of the elect did not present itself to him as an organized community of the saved, moulded by particular commandments. It is true that the men of Qumran also realized that God alone knows his own and that membership of the community of the saved did not automatically guarantee salvation. But they could not imagine how salvation could be possible outside, away from the holy service which they rendered. In the community of Qumran we see for the first time a 'church', a communion of saints, the elect at the end of time. Israel was never a 'church' and never claimed to be one; it saw itself as the chosen people to whom God revealed himself through his guidance and leadership in history. In Qumran a dividing line was drawn right through the middle of Israel's historical entity: it is not the people as a whole who are chosen, but the individual; it is not the people as such who can be the Israel of the covenant, but the community of the saved, the assembly of the elect. Through the withdrawal into the desert and the creation of a monastically ascetic community this dividing line became outwardly visible. Because of his attachment to the already existing community, the teacher of Qumran lacked the liberty and pleasure in creation which radiates from Jesus' parables of the kingdom. Nor could he describe the contrast between present and future with the same clarity; for the continuity of the community, which endured and kept its own identity, had to be taken into particular account. Hence the Qumran allegory describes a state, a power resting within itself, emphasis lying on its capacity for resistance and steadfastness in the cataclysm of the last days. In Jesus' parables, on the other hand, there is action; both God's behaviour and the conduct of the man who trusts in him are depicted.

In fact, fear of the worldly and profane prevented the Qumran writings from describing eschatological existence in scenes taken from everyday life, as Jesus did. If the Qumran community is for once described with any imagery, this is so decked out and elaborated with biblical references and concealed and open allusions to scripture, that its own character hardly emerges at all.

Duty towards one's neighbour, which is especially stressed in Jesus' parables, is in Qumran also prescribed by commandments and is in essence confined to the sphere of the community. As we have seen, love towards God and one's neighbour is the essence of Qumran piety too. But between the devout and God stands the scriptural precept, between the devout and his neighbour the order of the community. There are really no unforeseen encounters, like that described, for instance, in the parable of the good Samaritan, no spontaneous decisions to serve others, no situation ethics. Narrow limits are drawn round individual responsibility. The question of who one's neighbour is is regulated by a strict order of precedence.

The individual about whom Jesus speaks in the parables, on the other hand, has no safeguards and is not confined by any religious, national or social order. Or his safeguards have disappeared and he is swept away, for a time, from the compulsions and securities of such an order: the servant often acts as the steward of his master's whole property, or his master is absent. The Samaritan in the parable is in the midst of the Jews; the priest and the Levite come upon the wounded man far from the temple; it is quite alone that the labourer and the merchant decide to take the risk of acquiring the costly treasure.

Although the parable is missing in Qumran, the rabbis

often used this narrative form. The public preaching of Rabbi Meir is said to have consisted of a third *halacha* (expounding of the law), a third *haggada* (devotional matter) and a third parables.[36] These parables are closely related even in form to the parables of Jesus which have come down to us. For example, Rabbi Gamaliel II, who taught about the end of the first century AD, is recorded as beginning a parable as follows: 'I will tell you a parable. With what shall I compare this? It is like an earthly king who went forth to war . . .'[37] Jesus could begin a parable very similarly (cf. Matt. 11.16; 18.23) and, like the rabbis, he illustrated God's actions through the behaviour of a king or powerful lord (cf. Matt. 18.23; 22.2; Luke 14.31-32). In other ways, too, there is much that is familiar in the storehouse of rabbinic parables. But the kingdom of God as eschatological power does not take a central place there and there is no parable which describes God's joy over the returning sinner. It is rather when the soul of an innocent person appears[38] or when an evil-doer is destroyed[39] that there is rejoicing in heaven.

Finally, the parables of Jesus are closely linked with his activity and take on a deeper meaning in that light. In Qumran the community was accounted to be the place where God's eschatologically effective power was already present; hence it is veiled in allegory. But in the Gospels, too, there is a mystery of the kingdom of God. It is mentioned in connection with the parables of Jesus, although it seems to contradict their intention and hence presents us with a difficult problem. Mark says on the one hand that Jesus preached openly about the kingdom, using parables so that people could understand him (4.33); on the other

---

[36] Babylonian Talmud, *Sanhedrin* 38b.
[37] Mekilta 68a, Par. Jethro 6.
[38] Babylonian Talmud, *Mo'ed Qatan* 25b.
[39] Siphre Numeri 18b, para. 117 (37).

hand, he makes Jesus declare that the purpose of the
parables was to conceal the secret of the kingdom so that
outsiders might see and not perceive and might hear without understanding (4.12). This latter saying, stumbling-block
as it is, is generally attributed to the Christians, for they did
in fact find many parables mysterious and interpreted them
allegorically. But could not Jesus, too, have spoken of the
uncomprehended mystery of the kingdom?[40] And what
could this mystery then have been? Nothing less than the
fact that the rule of God has dawned in Jesus' words and
work and is already present in his person.

(c) *The Miracles of Jesus*

It is certain that Jesus performed miracles, healing all
kinds of sickness; that fact can be deduced even from the
Jewish polemic which called him a sorcerer. The expulsion
of unclean spirits is frequently mentioned in the Gospels and
miraculous healing, so alien to our way of thinking, must be
regarded as particularly characteristic of Jesus. What does
this mean, and in what relationship does it stand to Jesus'
preaching about the coming of the kingdom?

Belief in unclean spirits, or demons, who enter into
people, leading them to do evil or attacking them with severe
illnesses, was widespread in late Judaism and is also clearly
present in the apocalyptic writings. In Qumran it served to
justify a pessimistic view of the world. How did a divinely
created world come to be characterized by evil? Why are
injustice and lies in the ascendancy, although everyone
knows what is right and loves the truth? The answer is that
God created a good and wonderfully ordered world. The

[40] This is the view of Jeremias, who remarks on the antiquity of
the saying. But Mark did not understand it rightly, and wrongly
associated it with the parables (op. cit., pp. 14-18).

motion of the heavenly bodies, the alternation of day and night, the world of plants and animals, the distribution of peoples throughout the world – all this points to God's creative power, wisdom and goodness. But God also called into being two opposing spirits, the spirit of truth and the spirit of error, so that man might have the power of choice and be able to decide between them. It is possible to tell from every man's characteristics (which are the fruits of his actions) whose spirit's child he is. Through the rule of the two spirits, mankind is divided into two classes – the children of truth and light and the children of error and darkness. The superhuman realm is correspondingly divided into two camps. Since the fall of some of the angels (Gen. 6.1-4) there is between heaven and earth an anti-divine kingdom, which is ruled by Belial, the devil. He is the lord of the demons and employs them according to his purposes. This metaphysical dualism will only end in the last days. The War Rule tells how the armies of the Gentiles and the ungodly will be destroyed in a holy war and how the kingdom of the devil will be simultaneously blotted out. The Community Rule, however, promises that God himself will baptize the elect with the Holy Spirit, rooting out all spirit of error from them (4.20-22). Exorcism thus counts as an eschatological act and as God's peculiar work (cf. also *Thanksgiving Hymns* 3.18; *Book of Mysteries* I.1, 5).

Jesus' expulsion of demons must be interpreted against this background. Today the miracle stories in the New Testament, and especially Jesus' acts of exorcism, are often quietly ignored. The enlightened person, familiar with modern scientific methods, is embarrassed by them; for it is here more than anywhere else that the gulf between the ancient interpretation of life and the modern outlook is particularly wide. The Jesus of the Word is proclaimed as significant, but the Jesus of the miracles remains an alien figure set against a dark backcloth. Yet without the miracles, Jesus' acts and the message of the evangelists are incomplete in the extreme. For it was not so much through his words as through his miracles that Jesus showed that, in his person, the rule of God was a present reality.

The Qumran community remained confined to the defensive in the battle against evil spirits. The aim was to stand fast and to resist the wiles of the devil and his satellites with one's whole strength. Attempts were made to keep them in check by curses (*War Rule* 13.4-5); the 'sons of darkness' whom they dominated were also condemned by the anathema of the community (*Community Rule* 2.4-10). Yet satanic influence was felt, the isolated individual being thought to be in special danger. But he found refuge in the Law, accepted in a contrite spirit (*Damascus Rule* 16.5) and then in the community in which these divine precepts were truly lived and taught (*Thanksgiving Hymns* 6.25 ff.); finally, 'the children of light' relied on the support of God and the angel of his truth, Michael (*Community Rule* 3.24).

Jesus, on the other hand, did not remain on the defensive. He had no sheltering camp and was surrounded by no community of the elect; nor was the Law for him a bulwark behind which one could take refuge against the devil. He therefore went over to the attack. Since not only sin, but also all disease was to be laid at the door of the devil and the demons, he interpreted his miracles as victories over evil and a decisive break-through into the devil's realm.

Such victories over the devil and the demons proclaim that the divine rule is being realized, that God's power on earth is beginning to be effective. Redemption from evil and the coming of the kingdom of God coincide in time (Matt. 6.10-13). Hence Jesus could say, 'If it is by the Spirit of God that I cast out demons, then the kingdom of God has come upon you' (Matt. 12.28). We are reminded once more of what the Community Rule has to say about the decisive activity of God: he himself will banish every spirit of error, and he will do so at the end of time and through his holy spirit. From this point of view, Jesus, the exorcist anointed by the spirit, acted as God's eschatological proxy. His miracles are signs. Their significance is not exhausted in the incomprehensible act of healing itself. They point rather towards a still mightier event, proclaiming the temporal revolution that is in progress; with them the light of the last days falls upon the still darkened world. It is certainly only a beginning. Evil has received its sentence but is not yet annihilated; the divine rule is present, but only in Jesus himself, not yet universally in force.

It may be asked to what extent Jesus himself shared this belief in demons and the rule of Satan. Ernst Käsemann thinks that in exorcizing evil spirits Jesus did not act as 'a magician, believing that the world is literally bedevilled (thus subscribing to a metaphysical dualism)', but 'as one who knew the evil of the human heart and its demonic power and took possession of this heart for God. It is certain that Jesus did not put forward any metaphysical dualism – if he had done, how could he ever have been portrayed as a teacher of wisdom? – and was conscious of being sent not to fight the devil but to minister to man'.[41] This judgment is correct in as far as the antagonism of the two spirits, as it is described in the Qumran Community Rule, cannot be extracted from a single passage in the Synoptic Gospels. But it must not be forgotten that this dualism has its monistic summit in God and that even in Qumran there is no diminution of man's responsibility for his actions and for his evil heart. On the other hand, the debate over the expulsion of demons shows that Jesus, too, saw the devil as the lord of unclean spirits and compared him with the ruler of a king-

[41] 'The Problem of the Historical Jesus', pp. 39-40.

dom (Matt. 12.24). Exactly the same opinion was held in Qumran and in apocalyptic circles in general. And why should not Jesus, the exorcist, also have come to destroy the works of the devil? It is also questionable whether it is legitimate to see the service of man and the struggle with the devil as alternatives. The two are closely associated, both in late Judaism and in the New Testament.

Finally, it is false to separate miraculous healing from the forgiveness of sins. As is well known, the two are related to one another in the story of the man sick of the palsy (Mark 2.1-12 par.). Apparently without motivation, Jesus first promises forgiveness of sins to the sick man (vv. 5b-10); it is only after the intervention of the scribes that he performs the miracle. Following Bultmann, verses 5b-10 are generally judged to be a later interpolation: 'They arose because the church wanted to trace *its* right to forgive sins back to Jesus'.[42] But since both sin and sickness are to be put down to the account of Satan and his demons (*Community Rule* 3.20-24), the healing of the body would only be half a victory without the healing of the soul; indeed, measured by eschatological standards, the latter is the more important and an act peculiar to God himself (*Community Rule* 4.20-22). Above all, however, modern interpreters of the Bible should not fail to notice what the scribes in this story realized – that Jesus is here acting in God's stead (v. 7b) and in his strength, and does so in both cases, where he forgives sins and where he heals. For he is doing precisely what the author of Psalm 103 testifies of God himself: 'Who forgives all your iniquity, who heals all your diseases' (v. 3). This verse brackets both Jesus' actions together and makes it clear that the warrant to heal can be the proof of the right to forgive sins (Mark 2.10).

[42] Rudolf Bultmann, *The History of the Synoptic Tradition*, Oxford 1963, p. 15.

If one considers the holy war of the end-time, as it was prepared for in Qumran, Jesus' struggle with the devil acquires perhaps an even greater significance. The War Rule shows how alive the Old Testament tradition of the Holy War was in late Jewish circles. In Qumran it was taken over completely, brought into line with the up-to-date equipment and tactics of the day and interpreted in the light of eschatological expectation. Nothing of this kind is reported about Jesus. He created no army camp, set up no holy militia and devised no instructions for equipment and manoeuvres in an eschatological world war. The Gentiles were not to him *per se* the opponents of the divine rule. On the contrary: Jesus could see many coming from the east and the west and sitting down as guests at table in the kingdom of God (Matt. 8.11). Even the sinner seemed to him not an adversary but the object of God's special concern; and in spite of the call to repentance, which presupposes freedom of decision, Jesus considered the devil to be a dangerous power enslaving men. Hence it is doubtless correct when the evangelists show Jesus in a violent struggle with the devil and the demons, while coming to men as physician and saviour, servant and helper. In this fight against evil Jesus no doubt took up the tradition of the Holy War. He gave it a fresh interpretation, spiritualizing and thus carrying it to a conclusion. Jesus did not dream about the time when the armies of the nations would be suddenly destroyed at the end of history, but saw God's eschatological display of power in the healing of the sick and the salvation of sinners. There was for him no question of what was permitted – to save life or to kill (cf. Mark 3.4).

What was the meaning of the miracle stories for the first Christians? Why was Jesus represented as Saviour? It is in the earliest Gospel that miracles occupy a particularly prominent place. If we follow Bultmann, for Mark Jesus was

not so much a preacher of repentance and a teacher of the
Law as the 'divine man', the Son of God in earthly form.
The impulse towards such glorification came from the Hellenistic world; Hellenism also provided substantial help
towards presenting Jesus in these terms, in the form of
miracle stories.[43] Bultmann points to the material collected
by Ludwig Bieler: classical antiquity was familiar with the
'divine man', endowed with supernatural powers, who did
all kinds of miracles. The spirit of God gave him incredible
knowledge and insight into human hearts, and in addition
the power to drive out demons, heal the sick and occasionally even to frustrate the fate of an early death.[44] Bultmann
also detects this type of 'divine man' in Mark's picture of
Jesus.

Is this view correct? Was the Son of God in Mark, with
the miracles which he performed, depicted essentially along
Hellenistic lines? I doubt it. At this point, too, Bultmann has
overestimated Hellenistic influence. Quite apart from this,
the 'divine man' type seems to me to be an artificial construction,[45] but even if such a type did exist, the New Testament scholar should be much more inclined to look back to
the 'men of God' of the Old Testament. Bultmann wrongly
disputes the significance which the Old Testament tradition
must have had for the miracles of Jesus.[46] His thesis is therefore usually modified today. Ferdinand Hahn allows that
the Palestinian Christians were influenced by the picture of
the Old Testament men of God and saw in Jesus the New

[43] Op. cit., p. 236.
[44] L. Bieler, *Theios Aner*, Vienna 1935 (reprinted Darmstadt
1967).
[45] Anyone who is not blinded by the mass of material in Bieler's
book will easily see that it does not always fit the 'divine man' type
very well. The designation appears only rarely, and individual
miraculous features do not make up a particular homogeneous type.
What, for example, does the divine swineherd of the Odyssey have
in common with Apollonius of Tyana and with Jesus and Paul?
[46] Op. cit., p. 230.

Moses; the Hellenistic Christians, he argues, took this interpretation of Jesus further with the help of the idea of the
'divine man' and made Jesus a mythical Son of God.[47] But
even this correction does not go far enough. We need not
dispute that the Jesus of the miracle stories accorded with
the hope of Hellenistic man, though he plays no part in
Paul, the apostle to the Gentiles. First, however, we must
look at the Marcan miracles in the light of the Old Testament tradition and Jewish exegesis, and then decide what is
left for Hellenism and its 'divine man'.

We cannot, of course, do this in detail here, not least
because there are sometimes a number of interwoven themes
in the miracle stories. While they present Jesus above all as
the second Moses, the tradition of the young David and the
prophets Elijah and Elisha have also had their various in-
fluences. When the men of Qumran wanted to strengthen
faith they conjured up the memories of Moses and David:
the annihilation of the Egyptians at the Reed Sea and the
victory over Goliath showed that God can bring about great
things through his chosen ones – why should that not be
possible now, in the end-time (*War Rule*, 11.1-10)? There
was a rabbinic belief that the second deliverer, the Messiah,
would be like the first, Moses, and the Christians, too, saw ɀ
prefigurement of Jesus in the miracles done by Moses (Acts
7.36-7).

According to Mark, the power by which Jesus did his
miracles is that of the Holy Spirit, which he had received at
his baptism (Mark 1.9-11). David, too, had once been
anointed with the spirit of God before he emerged as Israel's
helper: he was the man after God's heart (I Sam. 13.14;
Acts 13.22) and received the spirit as a permanent possession (I Sam. 16.13). The same thing is meant when, according to the account of the baptism of Jesus, the Holy Spirit

[47] F. Hahn, *Christologische Hoheitstitel*[2], Göttingen 1964, p. 295.

descends upon Jesus like a dove and the voice of God declares: 'Thou art my beloved Son; with thee I am well
pleased' (Mark 1.10-11; John 1.32, 34). David first proved
the power of the spirit at Saul's court, where he drove out
the evil spirit of the king (I Sam. 16.23); Mark likewise describes the expulsion of an unclean spirit as the first mighty
act of Jesus (1.21-28). Of course this first miracle is also akin
to the Elijah tradition, which appears in the presentation of
the first activity of Jesus in his immediate homeland both in
Luke (4.26) and in John (2.4). When her son lay dead, the
widow of Zarephath believed that Elijah had come to destroy her house and spoke out against him: 'What have you
to do with me, O man of God?' (I Kings 17.18). In the same
way, the demon in Mark 1.24 says: 'What have you to do
with us, Jesus of Nazareth? Have you come to destroy us?[48]
I know who you are, the Holy One of God?' With the Old
Testament word of division the demon reveals the gulf
which separates God's plenipotentiary from the power of
darkness, which is also stressed in Qumran (*Community
Rule* 4.18).

The demon of Gadara attacks Jesus with the same words
(Mark 5.7). He is called 'Legion' because he represents a
whole host of demons in the land of the Gentiles (v. 9); after
they are driven out, this host goes into a herd of swine and
is hurled by them into the lake (vv. 11-20). What is the
reason for telling this strange story? Mark attached it to the
miracle of the stilling of the storm (4.35-41), which throws
light on its meaning. For in stilling the storm and saving the
disciples Jesus performed a similar act to Moses, who
divided the waters of the Reed Sea and brought Israel safely

[48] The demons are corrupters by nature. Compare the story of the
demon Agrat in the Babylonian Talmud, *Pesahim* 112b-113a, according to which each of myriads of avenging angels had the power
'to corrupt'. With the appearance of Jesus their time of corruption
draws near.

to the other side. Destruction broke out on Israel's oppressors, the Egyptians; the same thing happens at Gadara, where Jesus drowns the demons, man's eternal enemy. This combination of the two miracles is confirmed by Jewish prayer: At the time of Jesus, Jews acknowledged daily before God: 'Thou didst divide the Reed Sea and the godless were swallowed up; thou didst lead thy beloved ones over, but the waters covered their oppressors.'[49]

In the same way, the happenings at the Reed Sea provide the most meaningful background for Jesus' walking on the water (Mark 6.45-52);[50] this is also true of the additional theme of Peter's sinking (Matt. 14.28-31).[51] This reference is again confirmed by the context. For the miracle of the walking on the water always belongs with the feeding of the five thousand (Mark 6.30-44 par.; John 6), which is intended to recall the feeding of Israel with the manna (John 6.31). Similar miracles are also recorded of Joshua, Elijah and Elisha (Joshua 3.14-17; II Kings 2.8-14; 4.42-44), and the evangelists must have been thinking of the healing miracles of the two latter when they told of Jesus' miraculous healing of sick children. In his healing of the blind, the deaf and the lame, Jesus fulfils the Old Testament expectation of the time of salvation (Isa. 35.3-6; 61.1-2).

Despite this, it must not be assumed that the miracles of Jesus are merely symbolic poetry, traditions told in a vivid

[49] In Morning Prayer after the *Shema'* (W. Staerk, *Altjüdische Gebete*, in Lietzmann, Kleine Texte no. 58, p. 7). The word for 'godless' (*zedīm*) could easily be connected with the term for demons (*šedīm*).

[50] Like the miracle of the stilling of the storm, the miracle of the walking on the water is a 'transition story'. It is a question, as at the Reed Sea, 'of going over' (Mark 4.35 par.; 6.45 par.; John 6.17).

[51] Compare rabbinic exegesis, according to which Nahson, the son of Aminadab, was the first Israelite to go into the Reed Sea; he is said to have sunk in the waves and Moses' rod, which divided the sea, saved him (Mekilta on Exodus, Tractate Beshallah 6, ed. Lauterbach, vol. 1, p. 235).

way. The testimony of Josephus shows how vivid the biblical miracles were at the time of Jesus and how avidly their
repetition was awaited. About fifteen years after the death
of Jesus, Theudas led a great crowd of people to the Jordan
and promised that he would divide the river and lead them
safely over; before this happened, a squadron of Roman
cavalry appeared and killed many of them (*Antiquities* 20.
97-98). A few years later a similar misfortune happened
when an Egyptian ascended the Mount of Olives and promised that from there he would break down the walls of
Jerusalem (*Antiquities* 20.169-171). 'Spirits of delusion' led
crowds out into the wilderness where God was to show them
'signs of freedom'; again the Romans arranged a massacre,
as Felix, the procurator, saw such undertakings as a signal
for rebellion (Jewish War 258-260). Such a verdict is quite
understandable, as the 'signs of freedom' were meant to
prove to the people that the hour of deliverance had come
and that God had decided on the fall of Rome. This proof
could only succeed if the people saw with their own eyes the
miracles of the time of Moses and Joshua: going through
the water, being fed in the wilderness and the destruction of
the city occupied by the enemy. Such miracles were 'signs'
of Israel's leader and deliverer sent by God; Jesus, too, was
therefore asked for a 'sign from heaven', a legitimating,
divinely sent 'sign of freedom' (Mark 8.11).

Are the Gospel miracles meant to be such 'signs of freedom'? The answer must be 'no'. It is true that they showed
Jesus to be the deliverer of Israel and the second Moses, but
he did not, as was expected, shake off the yoke of foreign
rule. In the face of the coming kingdom of God, the true
enemies of Israel are not political powers but the devil and
his agents. The story of the Temptation already guards
against a misunderstanding of the work of Jesus in a
political sense; here Satan represents the popular expecta-

tion of a Messiah (Matt. 4.3-10). In a similar way, Mark
records the end of a legion of demons, not of a Roman
legion. The existential and eschatological meaning of this
mythical event is further clarified by passages from Qumran.
In Qumran, the turn of the ages is marked by the fall of the
devil's rule; the demons will be imprisoned in Hades behind
bolts and bars (*Thanksgiving Hymns* 3.17-18). In Jesus'
miracles the lake symbolizes the power of death and corruption which, with the final judgment, threatens not only
demons, but men. This is also true of the stories of the stilling of the storm and the walking on the water. They are
therefore not 'nature miracles', as is sometimes thought, but
victories over death and the devil, from whom Jesus
snatches the prey which they thought to be safely theirs.[52]
Both, therefore, serve the same eschatological end, to which
the miracles of healing are also directed. In the latter the
healing of physical hurt is seen as only a partial aspect,
which stands in the foreground. It is much more important
that the person who is healed is snatched away from corruption and placed in the sphere of salvation, and accepted
completely, soul and body, by God. Jesus' healing miracles
thus have a similar significance to John's baptism of repentance, which is meant to be an outward sign of forgiveness, of the acceptance of the sinner. The same is true of the
feeding of the five thousand, in which Jesus anticipates the
feast in the kingdom of God for those who look for him.

When they were transferred to Jesus and consequently
given new interpretations, the Old Testament miracles were

[52] Jesus' walking on the water proclaims his victory over the
powers of chaos, which can also be represented by wild beasts.
Compare Thanksgiving Hymns 3.17: the demons are creatures of
the adder – the old serpent; in Thanksgiving Hymns 5.6-7, lions
represent the powers of chaos. According to Luke 10.19, the disciples who drove out demons had authority to tread on snakes and
scorpions; according to Ps. 91.13, anyone who trusts in God can
walk on lions and adders, and trample lions and dragons underfoot.

detached from their link with past history and the people of Israel as a whole. As eschatological events they illuminate the existential situation of every man: his lostness in the world and his deliverance by God. Even in the Old Testament, the happenings at the Reed Sea are sometimes interpreted mythically, as a victory over the power of chaos, and thus made an event of the present which points to the future. This approach is strengthened in apocalyptic, and applied to the individual. In Qumran, we find the illustration of the lonely sailor on a stormy sea to describe man's lostness and his fallenness, under the sway of death and the devil (*Thanksgiving Hymns* 6.22-25); conversely, salvation already experienced is praised as deliverance from Sheol (*Thanksgiving Hymns* 3.19-20). These eschatological alternatives of total damnation or eternal salvation are characteristic of the self-understanding of the apocalyptists of Palestine. True, Hellenism, too, had its notions about possessed men. But the demons do not appear, as they do in Palestine, as a plague on mankind, and exorcism is pictured as a pleasant entertainment rather than as a sign of God's deliverance.[53] The Greek miracles lack the dominant characteristic of the biblical miracles and the 'signs of freedom', namely the symbolism which points beyond the act itself and even the miracle worker, and calls forth faith in God the deliverer. This is particularly true of the eschatological situation of which the men of Qumran and the first Christians were conscious. Yet here again, we find the difference which has already been indicated. For the Qumran believer the community represented a miraculous haven of safety (*Thanksgiving Hymns* 3.21-22; 6.25-27); for the Christian, salvation is guaranteed by fellowship with Jesus.

---

[53] Compare the Hellenistic reports of the expulsions of demons in Philostratus IV 20 (Apollonius of Tyana) and Josephus, *Antiquities* 8.46-49 (Eliezer before Vespasian).

What is the origin of this concentration of faith on a person? For Mark, the miracles of Jesus have a messianic significance; they reveal Jesus as the anointed one and the divinely sent deliverer of the end-time. This is certainly an appropriate interpretation of the work of the historical Jesus: he visited and saved what was lost. But is his claim also rightly understood: did Jesus in fact set out to be Messiah and Son of God?

(d) The Response to the Activity of Jesus

(i) The disciples

Jesus was an itinerant teacher who was accompanied by a group of disciples. This does not necessarily indicate a rabbi. Josephus writes about an Essene, Judas, who made his appearance c. 100 BC; he was surrounded by a throng of disciples who wanted to learn from him the art of prophecy, i.e. probably the prophetic interpretation of the scriptures (*Jewish Antiquities* 13.311). A group of this kind may have been the nucleus of the monastic community in Qumran. Josephus asserts that he himself was for three years the disciple of a man called Bannus, who lived as an ascetic in the desert, feeding and clothing himself from what grew there and frequently performing ritual washings in cold water (*Life* 11-12). Bannus is reminiscent of John the Baptist, who must also have had an established circle of followers, since after his death, and far from Palestine, men claimed to be his disciples (Acts 19.1-6). Finally, the pupils of a rabbinic teacher sat on the ground at his feet in order to absorb the wisdom he handed down with their 'eyes, ears and every member'. Often such pupils adopted not only the teaching but also the way of life of their master: they imitated him, served him and shared his scanty meals.[54] But

[54] B. Gerhardsson, *Memory and Manuscript*, pp. 182-3.

the community life which turns the pupil into the disciple
and the teacher into lord and master is most clearly distinguishable in Jesus' disciples, and before that in Qumran.
Whoever belonged to the holy men of the Qumran monastery had left father and mother, wife and children. All that
he had was turned over to the steward of the order's property and thus given to the community – indeed put at the
disposal of God himself. For in the moment when it was
removed from the secular economic framework, which was
devoted to selfish interests, it counted as consecrated, a
sacrifice on the altar of God. The monk, too, had presented
himself as a living sacrifice, consecrating not only his money
but also his bodily and mental strength to service in the
community.[55] In return the community supported and cared
for him; he ate at the common table and prayed and con-
sulted together with his brethren.[56] In place of the physical
family whom he had given up he was now a member of a
new spiritual community, which also described itself as a
family.

Jesus' disciples were also united with him in a similar
community life. When Jesus called them they left everything, giving up their livelihoods and leaving their parents
(Matt. 4.18-22; 19.27; Mark 10.28-31). Separation from
family and home was hard. The Qumran teacher com-
plained that he had been banished from his country like a
bird out of the nest and that he had been driven from all his
relations and friends (*Thanksgiving Hymns* 4.8-9); Jesus
could say that the Son of Man had nowhere to lay his head
(Matt. 8.20 par.).

Jesus, too, replaced the physical family by a spiritual one.
He rejected the attempt of his mother, brothers and sisters to
fetch him home. Whoever did the will of God were his

[55] Community Rule 1.11-13; 5.1-3; 6.19.
[56] Community Rule 6.2-3; Jewish War 2.124-33.

brother, sister and mother (Mark 3.31-35) and God himself was the father of this family (Matt. 23.9). Like the Qumran monks, Jesus' disciples ate and prayed together. They lived from a common purse, from which they paid for the common meal (Mark 8.14), and Judas Iscariot, who carried the money-bag (John 12.6), was the steward of their property. Similarly, the disciples had a prayer of their own, given to them by Jesus, which was also a feature of John the Baptist's disciples (Luke 11.1-4). The common meal was a special expression of the close association of the group. As in Qumran, it was accounted the gravest breach of trust when any one who broke bread with the master rebelled against him; in both places such sacrilege is condemned in the words of Psalm 41.9.[57]

The behaviour of the first Jerusalem Christians shows how impressive the *vita communis*, and especially the common meal, with Jesus must have been: they, too, have their common prayers, the breaking of bread in their houses, turn and turn about, and the offerings of money acquired by selling property (Acts 2.42-47; 4.32-5.11). This 'communism of love' was the natural continuation of the community life founded by Jesus. The overflowing joy which accompanied the meal (Acts 2.46) was a demonstration of the living hope of the second coming of Jesus and the final communion with the exalted Lord. In Qumran the common meal already had an eschatological connotation; the seating order provided for places for the last of the High Priests and for the Messiah (Supplement to the *Community Rule* 2.11-14). Among the first Christians the messianic character of the meal was intensified. From early on it was called the Lord's Supper (I Cor. 11.20), through which the death of Christ was proclaimed until his coming (I Cor. 11.26).

[57] Cf. Mark 14.18-20; John 13.18 with Hymns of Thanksgiving 5.24.

What distinguishes the fellowship of Jesus' disciples from the community fostered in Qumran is, on the one hand, the joy which emanates from Jesus' message and from the victory over Satan and, on the other, freedom and open-mindedness towards the worldly order and towards worldly goods. There was no compulsion; the rules of discipleship were not, as it were, turned into a general and essential law. That is the explanation of the fact that the surrender of property in the primitive church is presented, not as a command, but as a free-will offering (Acts 5.4). This spirit of liberty stems from Jesus. True, he was unmarried, but he did not demand celibacy, rather stressing the purity and indissoluble nature of marriage. He was poor and had to ask for the *denarius* with the help of which he settled the question of the imperial tax (Mark 12.15-16); but compared with John the Baptist Jesus seemed to people a positive glutton and wine-bibber (Matt. 11.19). He forbade his disciples to fast, for his acts were a sign of the end-time and its accompanying joy, which he compared with a wedding feast (Mark 2.19). The community of the disciples was open towards the world.[58] Whereas in Qumran the banquet was only for the pure, the full members of the community, Jesus broke bread with everyone, even sitting down at table with the publicans and sinners, thus offering them the meal fellowship of the kingdom of God. Following the precedent of the priestly Torah, the blind, deaf, lame and mentally deficient were not admitted to the Qumran community, for an imperfect person cannot be used in the service of God (Supplement to the *Community Rule* 2.3-8; *Damascus Rule*, Fragment 15.15-17). Jesus, on the other hand, proclaimed that it is just such men as these that God will fetch to his great supper if the

[58] David Flusser sees a criticism of the ascetic piety of Qumran in the praise of the children of this world and the commendation to make friends with the mammon of unrighteousness (*Reschith Ha-Nasruth*, 1963, pp. 101-103).

righteous, with their other ties, are deaf to his call (Luke 14.18-24). Admittedly, the church soon adopted a practice reminiscent of Qumran when they forbade the catechumens to take part in the Lord's Supper.

Finally, it must be noticed that the disciples did not enter a community but followed Jesus the person. The term 'follow', which describes the complete attachment of the disciples to the earthly Jesus, has a firm place in early tradition, although it would be going too far to say that it was something new and unique from the very beginning.[59] For the rabbis also used the word to show the pupil's attitude to the teacher: he walks a few steps behind him and is his servant.[60] In the pre-Christian Damascus Rule, deriving from the Qumran circle, we already find the Hebrew *hālak 'aharē*, corresponding to the Greek verb *akolouthein*, which literally means 'to go behind someone'; there too it is used for attachment to the teacher (4.19-20). Admittedly, this concept does not seem to have been of importance in Qumran, being in fact in this one place applied to a false teacher. Instead of 'following', other verbs such as 'joining' or 'turning to' are used (*Damascus Rule* 4.3; 20.14-15); or obedience to the teacher is described as 'listening to his voice', which applies even when the teacher is no longer alive (*Damascus Rule* 20.28, 32).

The Old Testament background is important for the 'following' of Jesus, especially the story of how Elisha is called away from his plough by Elijah. Elisha's answer is expressed in the words, 'I will follow you' (I Kings 19.20). The same passage shows how stern and uncompromising the call of Jesus was. Elisha, sent back to his ploughing, was

[59] So E. Schweizer, 'Der Glaube an Jesus den "Herrn" in seiner Entwicklung von den ersten Nachfolgern bis zur hellenistischen Gemeinde', *Evangelische Theologie* 17 (1957), p. 7; G. Ebeling, *Word and Faith*, London and Philadelphia 1963, p. 235.

[60] B. Gerhardsson, op. cit., p. 183.

allowed to take leave of his father and mother (I Kings 19. 20). Jesus forbade it, for 'No one who puts his hand to the plough and looks back is fit for the kingdom of God' (Luke 9.62). Usually in the Old Testament 'following' is used in connection with the gods of the heathen or God himself. The demand to follow God was a problem for the rabbis; that emerges particularly from a passage in the Babylonian Talmud, *Sota* 14a, which sheds light on the New Testament in other respects as well. Following the exhortation, 'Walk after the Lord your God' (Deut. 13.4), the question is asked: how is it possible to follow God, since he is a consuming fire? The following of God is tested by service to one's neighbour. To follow God means to follow his behaviour towards men. Just as God clothed people (Adam and Eve), visited the sick (Abraham after the circumcision), comforted the mourners (Isaac, according to Gen. 25.11) and buried the dead (Moses in Deut. 34.6), so the godly man must do the same for his brother. According to Matthew's testimony, Jesus made the same demand, not on the basis of God's example but rather identifying himself with the neighbour who is served (Matt. 25.31-46).

Such evidence indicates what authority Jesus claimed for himself: he is the one to be followed, he himself receives the good done to the least of the brethren, and it is a man's attitude to him that determines the measure of the heavenly reward (Matt. 19.29; 25.34-40).

(ii) *The opponents*

In 1961, a book about the trial of Jesus[61] appeared which received much attention. In it the writer, Paul Winter, maintained the view that the Gospel presentation of Jesus' conflict with the Sadducees, scribes and Pharisees was not objective, being dominated by an anti-Jewish tendency. The

[61] *On the Trial of Jesus* (Studia Judaica, Vol. I), Berlin 1961.

evangelists saw everything from the viewpoint of Jesus' tragic death; their books 'grew in the shadow of the cross'. According to Winter's thesis, Mark already shows how from the beginning Jesus met with a growing resistance and animosity on the part of the Jewish spiritual and political leaders of the day; arrest, cross-examination and surrender to Pilate seemed the inevitable consequences of what was, even at the beginning, determined and inexorable opposition. Winter believes that though this account is understandable in view of the miscarriage of the church's mission to the Jews, it is a distortion of the true facts. The possibility must be contemplated that Jesus was arrested by Pilate and crucified as the result of a denunciation by the Sadducees; and no doubt some individual Pharisees were among his opponents. But there is no question of a fundamental difference between him and the Pharisees in general – in fact Jesus was a Pharisee himself. The disputes reported in the Gospels have their '*Sitz im Leben*', their situation, in the Christian church, not in the history of Jesus of Nazareth. No single opponent of Jesus is ever actually named by the evangelists. The opponent is always anonymous, the spokesman of a party. This fact betrays the antagonism of two groups – the Christian community and the unbelieving Jews. In other words, the adversaries of the church were described as the opponents of the historical Jesus, and points at issue in the later period were settled by the mighty word of the Lord of the church. Winter even calls in the Fourth Gospel as witness to the degree to which the situation coloured the picture of Jesus' opponents: the writer never speaks of the Sadducees at all, for the simple reason that at the time when he was writing his Gospel the Sadducees had ceased to be important and consequently were not numbered among the opponents of the Christians.[62]

[62] Op. cit., pp. 111-135.

Winter's analysis is penetrating in many respects. It *is* the
Sadducees and not the Pharisees who play a role in the story
of the passion; but that is already clear from Mark's Gospel,
as Winter himself shows.[63] It is also true that the evangelists
are dominated by an anti-Jewish attitude, especially Matthew. The author of the Fourth Gospel, on the other hand,
sees in the Jews not so much the members of the Jewish
people as the representatives of the world, with its hostility
to God. The anti-Jewish tendency is really cancelled out by
his dualistic cosmic view and his existential, kerygmatic
approach. From that standpoint it is almost a matter of
indifference whether the evangelist brings Pharisees or Sadducees, Caiaphas or Pilate on to the stage. Moreover, it is
questionable whether this Gospel can be separated from the
others by the time factor, for in fact the Sadducees had long
ceased to play an important part in Jewish politics even at
the period when Matthew and Luke were writing.

Do the disputes in the Synoptic Gospels really only belong
to the history of the Christian church? What, for instance,
could the church at Rome (almost certainly the birthplace
of Mark's Gospel) have had to do with the Sadducees, the
priestly aristocracy of Jerusalem, that it entered into a discussion with them over the resurrection of the dead (cf. Mark
12.18-27)? Such a debate fits as little into the Rome of the
period of the Jewish War[64] as does the Pharisees' question
about the first commandment. The Jewish-Christian dispute
was entirely dominated by one great problem – whether Jesus
was the divinely sent Messiah or not; that is clear from Acts
and it is confirmed by Justin's dialogue with the Jew Trypho.

At this point, too, it is useful to draw on the Qumran

[63] Op. cit., pp. 122-124.
[64] Eusebius, *Ecclesiastical History* II.5, puts the origin of Mark's
Gospel in Rome. Because of the references to war in Mark 13.7, the
time of composition is usually taken to be that of the Jewish War
(AD 67-69). See W. G. Kümmel, *Introduction to the New Testament*,
Nashville and London 1966, pp. 70 f.

texts, for they reveal much of the polemic of the Jewish parties in the New Testament period. They speak of many opponents and conduct their dispute with them with the greatest acrimony. But here, too, no names are given. Even the party names Sadducees and Pharisees, so familiar to us from the New Testament, are never used in the Dead Sea Scrolls, which increases the difficulty of identifying the opponents who are meant. The same is true of the rabbinic disputes, as they are reported in Mishnah, *Yadayim* 4.6-8.[65] In Qumran the prime enemy is the priestly aristocracy of Jerusalem – the same group that is referred to in the New Testament under the name of the Sadducees and the high priests. The enemy of the founder of the Qumran community is consistently referred to as the Wicked Priest – what would we not give to have his name mentioned in one single passage! Another group, clustered round the 'Liar', is generally described as 'seekers of smooth things'. This no doubt refers to the Pharisees. Their sincere attempt to adapt the commands of the Mosaic law to the changed conditions of their own time, and thus to make their fulfilment feasible, seemed to the men of Qumran a devil-inspired attempt at compromise. Such interpretation was heresy; the Pharisees seduced the people. 'They speak with mocking lips to the people and an alien tongue that they may cunningly turn all their works to folly', complains the man in the Thanksgiving Hymns to God (4.16-17). The only thing that can be hoped for is that the 'simple', the untaught masses, may have their eyes opened in time, so that they may find the way to the true Israel.[66] Such passages show that New Testament

[65] The Sadducees are mentioned as opponents of the Pharisees, although Rabbi Johanan ben Zakkai is introduced as a representative of the Pharisaic point of view.

[66] This is said above all in the *pesher* (interpretation) on the prophet Nahum (col. III. 4-6). Cf. J. M. Allegro, 'More unpublished pieces of a Qumran Commentary on Nahum (4QpNah)', *Journal of Semitic Studies* 7 (1962), pp. 304-6.

polemic does not originate in the Christian church. The reproach of hypocrisy which is levied against the Pharisees in the Gospels and has led to an unjustifiable identification of Pharisaism with hypocrisy (an identification by no means true to the historical role of the Pharisees) can be matched in the Qumran texts and also in the Talmud: even the Jewish king Alexander Jannaeus (103-76 BC) is said to have called the Pharisees 'falsifiers'.[67] This term of abuse does not belong to the Jewish-Christian controversy but to the struggle for 'truth', for the true interpretation of Holy Scripture; it does not point towards a Hellenistic community but towards Palestine, towards the historical Jesus. Jesus, too, sought passionately for the perfect will of God behind the letter of the Law; above all, he viewed the Pharisaic casuistical interpretation of individual commandments and the hedge of oral tradition as an obstacle on the road to the kingdom of God. For that reason alone he cannot himself have been a Pharisee. And the fact that he could set up precepts of his own about the Mosaic injunctions must have aroused the deepest resentment among all the Jewish religious parties. It must also have evoked the question: what did Jesus think about himself and what did he really claim to be?

An answer must be found to this question. How could Jesus behave in this way, so boldly interpreting the scriptures, entering into a fight to the death with Satan and the demons, and even maintaining that with his work the rule of God was practically speaking already in force? It is clear that for such a claim the category of rabbi, teacher of righteousness or prophetic voice, like John the Baptist, is totally inadequate. But what, then, did Jesus think about himself? What was his own interpretation? Was he simply a man who knew himself to have a divine commission, who

[67] Babylonian Talmud, *Sotah* 22b.

could represent God himself but without any particular office? This is sometimes maintained today.[68] But this answer ignores two facts. For one thing, the Qumran texts, and also the New Testament writings, show that a servant of God had to prove his credentials before the godly. He had to give a clear description of his commission in terms that met the requirements of scripture or tradition. The individual was not important; in Qumran he vanished entirely behind the office. The people who belong to the history of Israel are certainly named, as they are in the Bible. But, as has already been shown, this is true of none of the figures on the contemporary stage. They have titles describing an office or function: the Teacher of Righteousness, the Wicked Priest, the seekers of smooth things. It can be seen that even polemic clings to the title and colours it accordingly. And John, the voice in the wilderness, bears a title which he certainly did not give himself – he was the Baptist. The Gospels show how people puzzled over who John and Jesus really were and what they thought their mission was (John 1.19-23; Matt. 11.3); Jesus himself asked his disciples what people thought of him (Mark 8.27-28 par.). In answer, the mention of a particular office was expected, or the name of a man who was a particularly worthy holder of such an office: a prophet like Elijah or Jeremiah, John the Baptist or the Messiah (Matt. 16.14-16). It may be that one or other of these enquiries is not historical. But the fact that they are reported at all shows how much emphasis was laid on the need to formulate the divine commission clearly – to describe and justify it in the light of already existing ideas and concepts. And we know how Paul fought for the recognition of his apostolic status.

Moreover, the continuity of the Christian *kerygma* is in a

[68] E. Fuchs, 'Das Neue Testament und das hermeneutische Problem', *Zeitschrift für Theologie und Kirche* 58 (1961), pp. 212-3.

poor condition if we are able to see no more in the historical Jesus than a man commissioned by God, with neither office nor title. The church adorned the risen Lord with a multitude of titles and designations of sovereignty. Who gave it the right to do this if the historical Jesus did not claim any of these titles for himself or did not hold them to be in accordance with his mission? And how can our message then be made credible?

The problem of the bridge between the historical Jesus and the message of the church must constantly be borne in mind, although we shall now turn our attention to Jesus' end, his death on the cross.

THE QUESTION OF THE FOUNDATION
OF THE MESSAGE ABOUT CHRIST

(a) The Cross and Jesus' Messianic Confession

(i) Why was Jesus crucified?

THE fundamental fact to which the quest of the historical Jesus always brings us back is his death on the cross. Nowadays the liberal scholar is sometimes reproached with having no adequate explanation for this fact. How could the devout and lovable teacher of a higher morality possibly have been crucified?[1] But has the Bultmann school a better explanation? Why should a prophet and rabbi, a 'voice before the end', be more deserving of the cross than the liberal teacher of a higher ethic? It is not enough to point to Jesus' conflict with the Pharisees and the sovereign manner in which he dealt with the Law, tightening it up here, rescinding it altogether there. For no Jewish heretic ever died on the cross, and the Pharisees played no part in the trial of Jesus.[2]

Crucifixion was not a usual method of execution among the Jews.[3] It is therefore wrong to say that the Jews crucified

---

[1] Heinz Zahrnt, *The Historical Jesus*, London 1963.
[2] Paul Winter, *On the Trial of Jesus*, pp. 122-24.
[3] Jewish criminal law knew four methods of execution: stoning, burning, decapitation and strangling (Mishnah, *Sanhedrin* 7.1). It was customary to hang the bodies of executed blasphemers and idolaters on a stake (cf. Deut. 21.23 and Gal. 3.13: 'A hanged man is accursed by God'). This, however, was merely to make the punishment more of a deterrent. When the Hasmonean king Alexander Jannaeus took vengeance on his political opponents and had them

Jesus, even if the New Testament writers sometimes so express themselves. It was Pilate, the Roman procurator, who condemned Jesus to death and it was his soldiers who carried out the execution (Mark 15.15-26). Crucifixion was a part of Roman law, being accounted the cruellest and most degrading method of punishment.[4] It was therefore reserved for the worst criminals and the most dangerous enemies of the state – the armed robber and the political insurgent, who was put on a level with the robber.[5] This Roman legal conception comes out clearly in the Gospel accounts. Two 'robbers' were crucified with Jesus (Mark 15.27). By this is meant two armed Jewish rebels; that is clear in the case of Barabbas, 'who had committed murder in the insurrection' (Mark 15.7). Accordingly, it is clear from the very fact of crucifixion that Jesus was executed as a political insurgent according to Roman law. In the inscription on the cross the verdict is explicit: Jesus of Nazareth was 'the king of the Jews' (Mark 15.26). Since the Roman emperor had to be acknowledged as the lord of Judaea (cf. John 19.15), a 'king of the Jews' was bound to be condemned as a rebel (or 'robber') and crucified. There can be no doubt that here the Gospel account is giving the unvarnished historical facts. For what stamps Jesus as a common criminal according to Roman justice cannot be ascribed to any apologetic or dogmatic viewpoint, particularly if Mark wrote his Gospel in Rome.

---

executed in gruesome ways, the author of a commentary on Nahum composed at Qumran remarked: 'He hanged men alive, something that had never before happened in Israel.'

[4] Cf. Cicero, *Pro Rabirio* 5.16; *In Verrem* II, 5.64.165; Tacitus, *Histories* 4.11; Josephus, *Jewish War* 7.203; also J. Blinzler, *Der Prozess Jesu*², 1955, p. 177, and Paulus, *Sententiae* 5.17.2: *summa supplicia sunt crux, crematio, decollatio.*

[5] Paulus, *Sententiae* 5.22.1 = *Digest* 48.19.38, para. 2: *auctores seditionis et tumultus vel concitatores populi pro qualitate dignitatis aut in crucem tolluntur aut bestiis obiiciuntur aut in insulam deportantur.* Quoted in M. Hengel, *Die Zeloten*, Leiden 1961, p. 33.

By the king of the Jews was meant the Messiah who, at the call of God and anointed with the spirit of wisdom and strength, was to lead the forces of victory in the war for the liberation of Israel at the end of history. Thus Jesus met the fate of a pretender to the messianic title and his trial is presented in the Gospels as a messianic trial. According to Mark 15.2, Jesus answered the question whether he was the king of the Jews in the affirmative; he did so again when the high priest put the same question to him (Mark 14.61-62).

We are certainly bound to enquire whether it is not the faith of the church that is speaking at this point. Was it not formulating its own belief in Christ as the confession of Jesus, thus anchoring its creed in history? If the answer is 'yes' to this question, then Jesus was wrongly accused of messianic pretensions and was unjustly executed. That, in fact, is the general opinion today. In Germany especially there is widespread acceptance of the theory which William Wrede expounded in 1901: the historical Jesus never saw himself as the Messiah or claimed to be so; it was only the events of Easter that aroused in the disciples the belief that the risen Jesus must be the Christ.[6] Wrede's theory has meanwhile been examined and confirmed by the form critics, who point out that in the oldest layer of tradition, Q, there is no messianic Jesus and no messianic title.

But the theory of the non-messianic Jesus leads to new difficulties and leaves important problems unsolved. For one thing, it casts a dark shadow over the trial of Jesus. The prosecution and the judge were guilty men. Jesus was suspected without cause, illegally arrested, and died the victim of a judicial murder. If things are looked at in this way the

* *Das Messiasgeheimnis in den Evangelien*, new impression 1963. For a critique of Wrede's thesis see A. Schweitzer, *The Quest of the Historical Jesus*[2], London 1954, pp. 338-48.

mistrust between Christians and Jews will be scarcely re-
movable and the church will hardly be brought fully to
acknowledge its debt to the Jews. We have already mentioned that the evangelists are not unprejudiced reporters of
the trial of Jesus; their bitterness against the Jews often
breaks through. Yet none of them dares to say that Jesus
was falsely suspected of being the Messiah and that he de-
fended himself against such a charge. On the contrary: the
testimony of the inscription on the cross that Jesus was the
king of the Jews agrees with the confession he himself made
before his Jewish accusers and the judge Pilate: What you
say is true – I am the Messiah!

A second problem carries even greater weight. If belief in
the Christ really only began at Easter, it must be asked:
'How can the appearances of the risen Jesus have suggested
to the disciples the idea that Jesus . . . was the Messiah?'[7]
Lazarus and the young man of Nain were raised from the
dead, but without ever being recognized as Messiahs. The
Easter faith in Christ is thus not an analytic judgment; the
raising of the dead does not necessarily involve an elevation
to Messiah. What made the disciples connect the two saving
facts and proclaim that God had made the risen Jesus 'both
Lord and Christ' (Acts 2.36)? The Norwegian New Testament scholar N. A. Dahl has recently given serious attention
to this problem. But he comes to the astonishing conclusion
that the disciples refashioned the false accusation of the
trial into a confession of faith. Thus Caiaphas and Pilate
become, surprisingly enough, the indirect originators of
christology!

We shall now see briefly how in fact Jesus' confession was
taken up and confirmed by the christological witness of the
church. Jesus knew himself to be the Messiah, making this
plain for the first time at his trial. We shall therefore first

[7] Op. cit., p. 343.

look at the trial of Jesus as it is reported in the earliest of the Gospels, and shall then turn to the Easter creed of the disciples as it is given in its pre-Pauline form in Rom. 1.3-4.

(ii) *Jesus' saying about the temple and the prophecy of Nathan*

Numerous scholars hold that the nocturnal hearing before the Sanhedrin or Great Council (Mark 14.53-65) is an unhistorical invention of the Christian church. For one thing, none of the disciples was present, and for another, according to Jewish law a capital crime could never have been tried at night, and least of all on the night of the Passover. Various things can be said against this view. First, the law and rules of procedure in Jewish courts at the time of Jesus are no longer precisely known. The treatise on the Sanhedrin in the Mishnah, which describes Jewish trial procedure, was written over a hundred years later; moreover, it gives the Pharisaic point of view, which differed considerably from the Sadducean conception. But it must in any case be pointed out that the night session described in Mark 14.53-65 would hardly have been a full session of the Sanhedrin, especially since this was not usually held in the house of the high priest. It must rather have been a committee which that night heard witnesses in an attempt to form a picture of the guilt of the accused; such a proceeding is mentioned in Mishnah, *Sanhedrin* 5.5. It was only on the following morning that the plenary session met and decided to deliver Jesus over to Pilate (Mark 15.1).

The objection that none of the disciples was a witness of the hearing is, of course, a valid one. But then Mark does not give a complete account of the proceedings. He confines himself to two points which were under discussion: Jesus' saying about the temple and his claim to be the Messiah. As the account of the crucifixion shows, these two facts im-

mediately became public and could therefore also have come
to the ears of the disciples.

Let us now look at the course of the examination. Many
witnesses appear, but their evidence does not agree (14.56)
and does not allow Jesus to be condemned. Some of them
state 'We heard him say, "I will destroy this temple that is
made with hands, and in three days I will build another, not
made with hands"' (14.57 f.). Here, too, the witnesses do not
agree. Now the high priest, who conducts the examination,
invites Jesus to answer the accusations (14.60), and, when
he remains silent, puts the question, 'Are you the Christ, the
Son of the Blessed' (14.61-62)? Jesus answers: 'I am: and you
will see the Son of man sitting at the right hand of Power,
and coming with the clouds of heaven' (14.62). The high
priest treats this confession as blasphemy and he causes the
death sentence to be pronounced (14.63-64; cf. Lev. 24.16).

The logical progression of these events is not clear. Albert
Schweitzer asks: 'How did the High Priest know that Jesus
claimed to be the Messiah? . . . Why was the attempt first
made to bring up a saying about the temple which could be
interpreted as blasphemy in order to condemn him on this
ground?'[8] It might be asked in addition: why was Jesus'
messianic claim accounted blasphemous?

The answer to this question can be found if the messianic
hope of late Judaism is examined; I myself found the clue in
a fragmentary Qumran text.[9] There the Word of God proclaimed by Nathan in II Sam. 7 is applied to the Messiah
and the godly of the end-time. In this prophecy David, who
is considering building a temple, is taught by the prophet
that God is in need of no such house. He will rather himself
establish a place for his people (7.10) and make a house for

[8] Op. cit., p. 391.
[9] Published by J. M. Allegro, 'Fragments of a Qumran Scroll of
Eschatological Midrashim', *Journal of Biblical Literature* 77 (1958),
pp. 350-54.

the king (7.11). What is meant is the house or dynasty of David. God will 'raise' one of the king's sons and establish his kingdom for ever (7.12). God will be his father and he shall be God's son (7.14); true, he may be chastened like a son but, unlike Saul, he will not lose the mercy of God for ever (7.15). This Davidic king shall build a house for the name of God (7.13), i.e. the temple. This divine saying proclaimed by Nathan became a highly fruitful source of tradition. From the earliest period it was constantly re-interpreted and applied to contemporary needs.[10] Indeed, in it is embedded the origin and legitimation of Israel's messianic hope.[11] It is no wonder, therefore, if this saying be-came a cornerstone in the eschatological expectation of Qumran, and was also used by the first Christians.

This saying shows how Mark wants his account to be interpreted. It brings out the whole point of the high priest's question: anyone who claims the messianic dignity must consider that according to scripture he must also be 'Son of the Blessed' – the son of God. It is not only his own honour, it is the honour of God that is at stake. A powerless person who maintains that he is the Messiah blasphemes Almighty God, and in the eyes of the Jews blasphemy is the worst of all crimes.[12] In spite of this, the captive Jesus says 'I am'. But

[10] Cf. Psalm 89.20-38; 132.11-18; I Chron. 22.8-10.
[11] G. von Rad, *Old Testament Theology* I, p. 310.
[12] According to Mishnah, *Sanhedrin* 6.4, blasphemers were hanged after stoning and thus branded as accursed. Cf. also Mekilta Exodus Bahodesh 7 on Ex. 20.6: if anyone has profaned the name of God, then neither his own repentance nor the great Day of Atonement can expiate his sin, but only the penalty of death, preceded by chas-tisement. The objection is usually made that blasphemy is only committed where the holy name of God is spoken 'clearly', i.e., as it is written (Yahweh=kethib) instead of as it is read (Adonai= Qere) (thus Mishnah, *Sanhedrin* 7.5). But this narrow definition is not assumed in the trial of Jesus, where even a false claim to be Messiah falls under the heading of blasphemy. Such a conception seems to underlie a note in the Talmud about the messianic pre-tender Bar Kosiba (*b. Sanhedrin* 93b): Bar Kosiba is said to have declared to the rabbis, 'I am the Messiah'. After this claim had been

he adds, 'You will see the Son of man sitting at the right
hand of Power'. In his answer Jesus, too, reverently avoids
using the name of God, replacing it by the paraphrase
'Power'; it is therefore far from his intention to pay insuffi-
cient reverence to the almighty power of God. On the contrary, his sitting at the right hand of God will reveal God's
power to the whole world; precisely that is the office of the
Messiah and the meaning of the messianic age. The present
helplessness of Jesus is not counter-evidence. For his installation in royal dignity, the beginning of his rule 'in power',
has not yet begun. But God will not tarry for long and then
everyone, even his unbelieving opponents, will see Jesus
enthroned beside God as king of the end-time and judge of
the world. The Nathan prophecy also permits an answer to
the question why the saying about the temple is brought up
at this messianic trial. For according to II Sam. 7.13, the
offspring of David, who has been established in his kingdom
by God, is to build the temple, and Zechariah repeated this
demand to David's descendant Zerubbabel (6.12-13). If the
Nathan prophecy is given an eschatological interpretation,
the building of the house of God is a messianic duty. Conversely, anyone who sets up to be a builder of the temple is
indirectly claiming to be the Messiah and the Son of God. It
is now clear why the high priest, when an examination of the
witnesses to Jesus' statement about the temple is at a dead-
lock, puts the direct question as to the messianic claim and
forces Jesus' confession.

Whatever one may think about the historical authenticity

---

shown to be false on the grounds of Bar Kosiba's unjust treatment
of people, 'they killed him'. The norm for the rabbinic assessment of
claims to be the Messiah was, following Isa. 11.3-4, an intuitive
knowledge of people and an uncorruptible judgment. This norm can
be seen to underlie the Johannine portrait of Jesus (compare John
1.23 with Isa. 11.2, and John 1.40-49; 2.24-25; 4.17-19, 29-30, etc.,
with Isa. 11.3-4 and the Qumran fragment 4QMess ar); it has
nothing to do with the Greek 'divine man'.

of the examination as reported by Mark, the fact that Jesus actually spoke the words about the building of the temple will hardly be seriously doubted. Six passages in the New Testament testify to it,[13] and if the saying sometimes seems obscure, that rather speaks in favour of its authenticity. The witnesses in the trial did not understand or reproduce it properly either; hence the contradictions and hence Mark's belief that they were false witnesses (14.57). For although Jesus announced that the temple would be destroyed (Mark 13.2), he never maintained that it would be destroyed by him. The very fact that Jesus purified the temple contradicts any such intention. For the man who intends to pull down the temple has no need to 'purify' it forcibly in order to give it once more the dignity of a house of prayer (cf. Mark 11. 15-17). The purification of the temple, incidentally, is an action which points to the authority of a messianic king, since, as the examples of David, Solomon, Jeroboam, Hezekiah and Josiah show, in ancient Israel the king was responsible for the sanctuary.

In another respect, too, Jesus' saying about the building of the temple is in need of explanation. Jesus did not mean a building in the sense of the splendid Herodian temple. It was rather the new, eschatological sanctuary not made with hands (Mark 14.53). Jesus thought of the community of the saved in the end-time, which he was able to describe as a true temple built up of living stones – a description which had already been used in Qumran, particularly in the interpretation of the Nathan prophecy.[14] The words about the temple therefore belong with Jesus' famous saying that he would build a church on the rock, Peter, which would not

[13] Mark 14.58; 15.29; Matt. 26.61; 27.40; John 2.19; Acts 6.14.
[14] The expression 'not made with hands' (Mark 14.58) will derive from here; it may come from Ex. 15.17 f., which is quoted in lines 3-4 of the fragment of the Eschatological Midrashim: the true sanctuary of the community of the end-time is 'erected by the hands of God'.

be swallowed up even by the gates of the kingdom of death (Matt. 16.18). And the Nathan passage explains the fact – by no means a matter of course – that Jesus confirmed Peter's acknowledgment of his Messiahship with the promise to build a church. For as the Messiah he had to build the eschatological temple of God, which he interpreted as the community of the elect.

(iii) *Jesus' messianic consciousness*

Consequently Jesus knew himself to be the Messiah. He admitted as much before Pilate (Mark 15.2), and it was Jesus' 'good confession' (cf. I Tim. 6.13) that the faith of the disciples took over. It is in the messianic consciousness and the messianic confession that the new, specifically Christian factor appears in comparison with Qumran. It is true that the Teacher of Righteousness also said that he had built God a 'church', [15] and this community also interpreted itself as a living sanctuary. But the Teacher of Righteousness never said 'I have built a living temple' and his community never professed that he was the builder of an eschatological sanctuary.

Jesus' messianic confession solves the problem of why he had to suffer death on the cross and also clears up the question, which is constantly raised, about the guilty persons in the trial. The Jews do play a part in Jesus' trial. They denounced him to Pilate, according to Josephus (*Antiquities* 18.64), and delivered him to the Gentiles, as is said in the prophecy of the passion in Mark 10.33. But must they be called guilty? The high priest who, according to Mark, conducts the examination acts perfectly correctly. He does not base his judgment on the contradictory statements of witnesses, but calls for Jesus' own acknowledgment. And it almost looks as if he wants to entreat Jesus to abandon his untenable, blasphemous claim. The guilt of the Jewish

[15] 4QpPs. 37.2, 16.

authorities consists at most in the fact that they measure Jesus' claim against their own messianic views. Jesus could not be the Messiah since God did not acknowledge him even in Jerusalem. But Jesus' own disciples made the same mistake. The Sadducees should have told themselves that Jesus was not a 'robber', a revolutionary, in the sense in which Roman law meant the word. But even this recognition would probably not have prevented them from proceeding against Jesus. For the messianic claim was *per se* dangerous to the state. Whatever interpretation was given to it by the claimant, among the people it could wake an echo which might result in rioting and insurrection. From a legal point of view, therefore, it is impossible to talk about the guilt of the Jewish authorities: Jesus was not falsely accused.

Nor does talk about Jewish guilt seem appropriate from the point of view of the Christian faith. Jesus' claim to be the Messiah is universal;[16] that is particularly evident when 'Messiah' is interpreted by the term 'Son of man'. The Fourth Gospel therefore deliberately describes the Jews as the representatives of the world and Jesus as the incarnate divine Word. People of all countries and eras appear as the enemies of God and his revelation in Christ; all are blind and imprisoned in their own dogmas. We are bound to confess with Paul and the first Christians that Jesus was delivered for our offences and was raised again for our justification (Rom. 4.25).

(b) The Response to Jesus' Confession: Easter and the Christological Creed of the Church

(i) The Gospel and the prophecy of Nathan

The hope that Jesus would be crowned in Jerusalem in

[16] See the article by G. Lindeskog, 'Der Prozess Jesu im jüdisch-christlichen Religionsgesprach', '*Abraham unser Vater*': *Festschrift für Otto Michel*, Leiden 1963, pp. 325-6.

glory as king of the end-time died with Golgotha. But after the risen Jesus had appeared to the disciples they acknowledged that God had made the crucified one Lord and Christ (Acts 2.36). That was the message which Peter proclaimed in Judaea and Samaria and which Paul carried throughout the Roman empire. Jesus is the Messiah; God's future has already begun; the new age has arrived.

What was suppressed on the cross, rose up at Easter in changed form. Quite unexpectedly God had confirmed Jesus' messianic claim and the disciples developed it in the light of Holy Scripture. As we shall now see, the Nathan prophecy again became the basic text. The disciples believed that through Jesus, son of David at the end-time, God had fulfilled his promise to set an eternally ruling Davidic king on the throne. Nathan's prophecy helped them to see the resurrection of Jesus as being also an exaltation, an installation in the kingly dignity of the Messiah; thus the christological meaning of Easter became clear. Belief in Christ was formulated in accordance with II Sam. 7.12-14 and thus established on the foundation of the scriptures.

In this way the problem of continuity finds a natural solution. The Nathan saying, having decisively influenced the Old Testament messianic expectation and also moulded Jesus' own messianic consciousness, now became the text which helped to interpret the events of Easter and to transform them into a Gospel. The Jesus of history and the Christ of the proclamation are thus linked by the eschatological event of Easter and the prophetic witness of the Old Covenant. The correctness of this thesis is evident from the opening verses of the Epistle to the Romans. There Paul presents himself as messenger of the Gospel which God had in the Scriptures already promised through his prophets (Rom. 1.2). The substance of this Gospel is Jesus who according to the flesh is of the seed of David and according to the spirit of holiness has been enthroned as Son of God, by virtue of his resurrection from the dead (1.3-4). He is the Christ and Lord of the church; from him Paul has received his apostolic office, which makes him messenger among the Gentiles and calls him to proclaim that salvation may be gained through obedient faith in this message (1.5). These sentences, in which Paul summarizes the whole of the Gospel and his own commission, must be more carefully examined and we should not shirk the effort of a closer exegesis. Three points are of particular importance:

1.   The Gospel is the message of Christ, for it is in Jesus Christ that God's grace reaches its goal. But it stretches far back into the history of Israel: what God calls his chosen apostle to preach in the Last Days (1.1) was long since proclaimed by his prophets (1.2). The apostles thus continue the work of the prophets and stand on the ground of Old Testament prophecy. Paul was undoubtedly thinking of this unity of the earlier word of God and the Gospel in its widest sense; but there is a passage in which the Old Testament's testimony to the Christ is particularly clearly expressed.

2.   It was this prophetic word which stamped the two following verses of Romans (1.3-4). In these the apostle quotes a christological creed which must be numbered among the oldest statements in the New Testament. The credal character is revealed by the solemnity of the form, with its two parallel sentences; the clumsy expression 'spirit of holiness' points to the pre-Pauline, Palestinian origin, as does the reference to the son of David, which otherwise plays no part in Pauline christology.

In the two parallel sentences the double mode of being of the Messiah is established: Jesus was the son of David – as far as human descent was concerned he belonged to the house of David; at Easter, however, he was installed as Son of God, whose being is determined through the Holy Spirit.

This second dignity is by far the more important. Paul shows this by the way in which he introduces the early creed, in the course of so doing describing its content: Jesus is 'his', i.e. God's, son (1.3a). The two original, parallel credal sentences are consciously formed on the pattern of the Nathan saying which, as in Qumran, is given a messianic interpretation. The ruler who is prophesied in this saying is also described as Son of David and Son of God. He is of the seed of David, a son of the king's body (II Sam. 7.12); in Romans 1.3 this accent on the physical descent is interpreted by the formula 'according to the flesh'. But he will also be the son of God, according to the promise given in II Sam. 7.14: 'I will be his father, and he shall be my son.' The dignity and the essence of the sonship are determined by the attitude of the father: God will guide and lead the future regent, chastizing him as a human father brings up his son (II Sam. 7.14). In the Christian creed the same facts could be described in the formula 'according to the Spirit of holiness' (Rom. 1.4). For what unites Father and Son and helps to make the divine control comprehensible is the Holy Spirit. The sonship is here rightly interpreted, even in the sense of the Old Testament conception of kingship. For with the anointing the king receives the Holy Spirit, which raises him above ordinary men, conferring especial power and wisdom and thus making him the ideal regent.[17]

3.   The Christian formula, however, contains more than the Old Testament idea can convey; on the other hand, the riches of the christological creed only become clear against the biblical tradition of the king. This is particularly true if

[17] The phrases 'according to the flesh' – 'according to the spirit of holiness' are not used in an un-Pauline way in Rom. 1.3-4 as a description of the earthly or heavenly spheres (against E. Schweizer, *Evangelische Theologie* 15 (1955), pp. 564 ff. and F. Hahn, *Christologische Hoheitstitel²*, Göttingen 1964, p. 253). They correspond to a description of descent and nature to be found elsewhere in Paul (cf. Rom. 8.5; 9.3, 5; I Cor. 10.18).

we consider the *act* by which the Son of David receives the dignity of divine sonship. Only God can confer this honour. He 'raises' the future ruler and sets him on the throne (II Sam. 7.12); at the enthronement the king of Israel is adopted by God and declared to be his son (Ps. 2.7). First of all, the christological creed remains within the framework of the Old Testament tradition. The disciples confessed Jesus, the son of David at the end of time, to be 'Son of God' because God 'has raised him up'; this act was performed at Easter. But the confession in Rom. 1.4 shows that the resurrection – or, more exactly, the 'raising' of Jesus is to be understood in two senses: 1. God has 'made Jesus rise' from the dead by restoring him to life; 2. God has 'raised' (= 'exalted') Jesus as king of the end-time and enthroned him as Son of God. The second interpretation of the 'resurrection' was possible because the living Christ had been seen in the Easter visions as the exalted Messiah, enthroned at the right hand of God. Easter could therefore be understood in the light of the prophecy of Nathan, in which the 'raising up' of the Son of David refers to his enthronement. The new and unusual element in the Easter message was something that seems obvious to Christians today: Jesus has been raised from the dead. Both elements, however, the enthronement of the Messiah and his resurrection from the dead, could easily be taken together by Jesus' disciples. First of all, they were both expressed by the same Hebrew verb, *heqīm* or *he'emīd*. Furthermore, the decisive eschatological saving act of God was to be a 'raising' in this twofold sense: God 'makes the Messiah rise' by endowing him with power and setting him on the stage of history, and he makes the dead 'rise' by setting those who lie in the dust on their feet. Finally, the fact that Jesus is raised from the dead and thus has his body changed into a heavenly one makes it possible for him to be exalted to heaven and appointed Lord of the angels.

The disciples' acknowledgment of Christ at Easter does not, however, exclude the possibility that the historical Jesus already knew himself to be Messiah. Easter was not a completely new beginning, a *creatio ex nihilo*. This is made quite clear by another phrase in the confession in Rom. 1.4: at Easter, Jesus was appointed Son of God 'in power'. The position over Jesus' messianic dignity is the same as that over the kingdom of God, which has already come to men through the defeat of the devil (Matt. 12.28) but has not yet been realized 'in power' (cf. Mark 9.1). Thus the earthly Jesus had already been anointed Messiah with the Spirit and worked in the power of this Spirit, but was enthroned and thus named Son of God only at Easter. One need only think of David, the father of Jesus according to the flesh: he was chosen and anointed king at a very early stage, but he had to wait a long time until he was raised to be king 'in power' (cf. I Sam. 16 and II Sam. 5).[18]

This christological confession, which is based on the Easter event and has been shaped by the prophecy of Nathan, can also be found in other writings in the New Testament. This indicates the important role it must have played for the first Christians, a role which has escaped New Testament interpretation right up to the present day. As in Romans 1.3-4, Paul's Gospel is summed up in II Tim. 2.8 in a creed-like formulation: it is about Jesus Christ, descended from David and risen from the dead.

Most instructive of all, however, is the way in which the Easter creed of Rom. 1.3-4 is taken up and developed in the Acts of the Apostles. This happens in the great inaugural speeches which Luke puts into the mouths of his principal

[18] In its original, probably Hebrew, form, the creed underlying Rom. 1.3-4 certainly did not present a 'two-stage' christology, but depicted the event of Easter in two clauses of equal weight. It may have run: 'God has raised up Jesus, the son of David, by the resurrection from the dead, and appointed him to be his son through the spirit of holiness.'

apostles Peter and Paul. In his Pentecost speech, the theme of which is the event of Easter, Peter makes David a prophet who foretold Jesus' resurrection from the dead and his exaltation to be heavenly ruler (Acts 2.25-35). The king had thus prophetically intimated the event to which the apostle Peter bears witness in his message (cf. Rom. 1.1-2). What enabled him to do that? In Peter's view, David could speak of the resurrection of Jesus because God had assured him with an oath that a physical descendant would sit on his throne (Acts 2.30-31). This statement can only be taken to be meaningful and conclusive if the promise on oath which it mentions is connected with the prophecy of Nathan and understood in the light of the creed in Rom. 1.3-4. Here, too, Jesus' resurrection is a 'raising up' in a twofold sense: enthronement and raising from the dead. In the view of the Christian interpreter, David had already understood Nathan's message in this way and in so doing had proved himself a true prophet. For he had seen and testified in the Psalter that God would gloriously fulfil his promise and bring about the 'raising' of the Messiah not only as an enthronement but also as a resurrection from the dead.

To prove this, Luke's Peter introduces two passages from the Davidic Psalms and joins them together by the prophecy of Nathan, which occupies a central place between them (Acts 2.30). It is preceded by Psalm 16.8-11, in which David announces that God will not leave his soul in the realm of the dead and will not permit his holy one to see corruption (2.25-28). This is taken as a prophetic testimony to Jesus' resurrection from death. But in these verses does not the king speak of himself and his own deliverance from death? Peter answers the question with a decisive 'no'. Such a superficial exegesis is refuted by the fact that David died and was buried: indeed his tomb is still there as evidence of this harsh reality (v. 29). In that case, the king in Psalm 16 must have spoken vicariously for someone else, the Messiah (v. 31). Why the Messiah? Because through the prophecy of Nathan David knew, first, that the Messiah will reign for ever and will therefore have to be delivered from Hades (II Sam. 7.13), and secondly, that the Messiah would be of his own seed, his own physical son (II Sam. 7.12). The king in Psalm 16 could therefore make himself a spokesman for the Messiah who was, as it were, 'still in his loins' (see Acts 2.30).

The second biblical passage which is taken to be David's testimony to Easter is Psalm 110.1, the most frequent quotation to appear in the New Testament: 'The Lord said to my Lord, Sit at my right hand, till I make thy enemies a stool for thy feet' (Acts 2.34-35). These verses confirm for Peter the other mode of 'raising up' which takes place at Easter, the enthronement intended in the prophecy of Nathan (II Sam. 7.12). Nathan's prophecy and Psalm 110 are taken together as prophecy and fulfilment: according to Psalm 110, the king sees how God discharges his promise given by Nathan and sets the future son of David on the throne. This son of David is Jesus, who is enthroned in heaven at the right hand of God and waits until his earthly enemies have been overcome and all points of the eschatological restoration have been fulfilled (see Acts 3.21). The apostle can bear witness that the eschatological act of God which was foreseen by David has already taken place. For he has been existentially involved in the saving event, he has personally experienced how God has 'raised' the Messiah, in two ways. At Easter the disciple saw the living Christ and so was made an apostle, the witness and messenger of his resurrection from the dead (Acts 2.32). At Pentecost he received the Holy Spirit which has made him certain of the reality of the exaltation of Christ and his own apostolic mission (2.4, 33).

Luke also makes his second principal apostle, Paul, proclaim the twofold 'raising' of Christ in a great speech (Acts

13). Like that of Peter, this speech is delivered before Jews, because the argument from scripture is comprehensible only to the Jews. The scene, however, is no longer Jerusalem but Antioch, a city in Asia Minor; there Paul already finds himself in the Diaspora, the area of the Gentile mission. In this way Luke means to show that the Gospel for the new, world-wide audience was no different from that for Jerusalem, and the Easter message itself is attested in Acts 13 in exactly the same way as in Acts 2.

David is again mentioned alongside the apostles as the present witness of the event of Easter (Acts 13.31): he is the prophetic herald of the promise which had been given to the fathers (v. 32), the divine servant of his own generation (v. 36). Here too the promise of the future son of David given to the king and interpreted in a messianic way forms the basis of his prophecy and the Christian argument from scripture. The quotation this time, however, is no longer the prophecy of Nathan itself but its variant Isa. 55.3, which is directed towards Israel and is therefore particularly significant from an existential point of view (Acts 13.34, prepared for in v. 32). Once again the picture of David, the prophet of Easter, is developed from this central point in two directions, like the two outer leaves of a triptych. Once again the resurrection of Jesus from the dead is attested by Psalm 16.10 (v. 35), while Psalm 2.7 fulfils the function of Psalm 110.1: at the enthronement the Messiah is named as Son of God (v. 33). Psalm 2.7 also belongs closely together with the prophecy of Nathan in the exegetical workshop of the first Christians. This is clear from Hebrews 1.5, where the unique worth of Jesus, the Son of God, is shown by means of the two passages.

Finally, Luke also constructed his Christmas story on the basis of the old creed in Romans 1.3-4 and the prophecy of Nathan. The messenger of Christmas sent by God is Gabriel.

In the Gospel which he brings to Mary, he proclaims that her child will be called the Son of the Most High, that God will give him the throne of his father David so that he is king for ever (Luke 1.31-32). This message is both a repetition of the prophecy of Nathan on an eschatological level and an anticipation of the apostolic preaching of Easter. For the character of the Messiah is determined by this twofold sonship: first, Jesus has David as his father, and will occupy his throne for ever; this is the promise made to the future son of David in II Sam. 7.12-13 and also stressed in Rom. 1.3. In Luke 1, Gabriel as it were takes the role of Nathan. Mary, who is betrothed to a member of the house of David (v. 27), occupies the place held by David in II Sam. 7: the Messiah will be her physical son, coming forth from her womb (compare Luke 1.31 with II Sam. 7.12). Jesus, however, is also to be the Son of God, as is promised in II Sam. 7.14, and, as in Rom. 1.4, the power of divine sonship is the Holy Spirit. What is new here is that according to Gabriel the Spirit is to take the place of human seed. The divine sonship is thus no longer based on adoption: it is defined on an analogy with physical procreation. At this point Luke goes beyond Old Testament and Jewish thought.

What the early church confessed in its message of Easter and Christmas is also read back into the activity of the earthly Jesus, but this time as a christological problem rather than as a christological creed. This happens in Jesus' question to the scribes: 'How can the Messiah be called son of David if David himself, guided by the Holy Spirit, calls him Lord?' (Mark 12.35-37, following Ps. 110.1). This question has made modern scribes rack their brains even more than those to whom the question was originally addressed. Why is it put at all, and what is the answer? It is, for example, assumed that this question betrays signs of the christological reflection of the first Palestinian community;

this community contrasted a heavenly Son of Man with the earthly son of David, perhaps even because Jesus' Davidic descent could no longer be demonstrated. Such an explanation is not, however, very satisfactory. How else would it have been possible for Jesus' Davidic descent to come to predominate so early, and especially among Palestinian Christians (cf. Rom. 1.3)? Others therefore prefer to argue that the pericope Mark 12.35-37 arose within the Hellenistic community; it is said to have conceived of a Son of God of supernatural descent as a counterpart to the son of David.[19] Jesus' question does not, however, dispute the Davidic descent of the Messiah, nor is the Messiah thought to be surpassed by a Son of Man or Son of God christology. Anyone who uses the prophecy of Nathan, interpreted in a messianic sense, as a key to this problem will recognize that the intention is not to put forward competing christological titles but rather to supplement one with another. For Jesus is David's son, as the traditional Jewish Messiah is always David's son. But as the eschatological Son of David, the Lord who sits on the right hand of God, he is at the same time the Son of God, and that goes to make up his unique status which surpasses that of his father David. The Christ taught by Peter and Paul knows the solution of the riddle which had been hidden from the scribes (cf. Acts 2 and 13).

(ii) *Easter vision and scriptural testimony*

Our discussion of the scriptural evidence seems highly theoretical. It almost looks as if the Christian faith were formed at the desks of the exegetes and is independent of historical reality. But that is not the case. The Easter experience remains basic – the encounter with the risen Christ, as this was later given credal form and developed in the

[19] R. Bultmann, *The History of the Synoptic Tradition*, Oxford 1963, pp. 136-7.

preaching of the Word. This encounter – the Easter vision – precedes all scholarly reflection; it is the basic datum, especially when the conversion of Paul is considered.

Only Paul has left us a personal testimony of the way in which the risen Christ appeared to him. He classed his own encounter with the glorified Lord with the visions of the disciples, putting it on the same level (I Cor. 15.5-8). The apostle certainly does not give us a detailed account; it is only in single, isolated sentences of his letter that he refers to his conversion and his Easter experience. In I Cor. 15.8 he mentions that Christ 'appeared' to him as the last of the apostles, and he stresses in I Cor. 9.1 that he has 'seen the Lord'. The vision, the sight of the risen Jesus, included the commission, the apostolic charge. Because he has seen the Lord, Paul claims the apostolic office for himself (I Cor. 9.1). In the passage discussed above, Rom. 1.5, he writes that he has received his apostolic office from Christ. Indeed he suggests that he received the commission to go to the Gentiles at the same time: 'It pleased God . . . to reveal his Son to me, in order that I might preach him among the Gentiles' (Gal. 1.16). Finally, the glad tidings of the Gospel were given at this first encounter; Paul did not receive them from men but through the revelation of Jesus Christ himself (Gal. 1.12).

How was Paul able to grasp the full implications of his encounter with Christ? The brief comments we have noted here show that Paul interpreted his experience in the light of the Old Testament. Indicative for him were the visions by which God called the great prophets to his service. The vision of Jeremiah is alluded to in Gal. 1.15 (cf. Jer. 1.5). The account of the calling of Isaiah must have been even more significant, especially when it is read in Greek and Aramaic translation. Just as Isaiah saw the Lord sitting on a throne high and lifted up (Isa. 6.1, 5), received God's commission and became his messenger (6.8), at the same time being given the message that he was to convey (6.9-13), so in the same way Paul had seen the exalted Lord and heavenly king, had been called by him as messenger or apostle, and had at the same time also received his Gospel. The 'Lord' now no longer meant God but Christ; the author of the Fourth Gospel could say that Isaiah had already seen Christ (12.41). He was enthroned in heaven as the ruler of the end-time and it is this that is the good news which must be carried to all men. Paul proclaims what he has seen. He knew that he had been sent to the Gentiles, because his Gospel suffered the same fate as did the message of Isaiah, which fell on deaf ears and closed eyes among the Jews (Isa. 6.9-10; cf. Acts 28.26-28).

A first answer is provided here to the question of the origin of the New Testament office of apostle. The apostles are Christ's messengers who have been called by visions of the risen Lord. They are modelled neither on the rabbinic delegate (*shaliah*, K. H. Rengstorf), nor on the heavenly messenger of gnosticism (W. Schmithals) but above all on the Old Testament prophet. In the conviction of early Christianity, the prophets had proclaimed the message of Christ beforehand and had thus performed for their time the service which the apostles were fulfilling after Easter (Rom. 1.1-2). Like the prophet, the apostle is a bearer of the Holy Spirit, which in New Testament times in particular is the spirit of prophecy. The 'raising' of the Messiah, his exaltation in heaven, is an event which remained hidden on earth, although it represents the turning point of the ages. For that very reason, messengers are needed who are sent by God and guided by the Holy Spirit: they are to proclaim to men things which no eye has seen and no ear has heard, but which God has revealed to his chosen instruments. The Gospel of the turning point of the ages also appears in a

Qumran fragment which has only been published recently (11QMelch). There it is said that the year of redemption will be ushered in with the enthronement of Michael in heaven as 'Melchizedek', king of righteousness, who will begin to judge the devil and his spirits. This will then be proclaimed by an evangelist anointed with the spirit; Isa. 52.7 is quoted as a proof. Now Paul quoted the same verse as a key text for the messengers of the Gospel of Christ (Rom. 10.15), and these messengers also proclaim the exaltation of a righteous king in heaven and the overthrow of the dominion of the devil.

(iii) *The christological titles*

In recent years a number of books have appeared in German on the christology of the New Testament. One cannot fail to be struck by the power and the profusion of early Christian credal formulations, especially as expressed in a whole series of christological titles. But the origin and inner unity of these titles remain a problem, as is indicated by the varied, indeed highly divergent, order in which they are listed in the various works. How could the first Christians confer all these titles on their Lord, calling him Christ, Son of David, Son of God, Kyrios, Saviour and Son of Man? And what is the thread which links them all together?

In the Old Testament most of these titles do not occur at all, and even the king of the end-time is not yet called the Messiah. But in late Judaism and among the first Christians there was a strong tendency to create titles. In doing so connections were made with biblical statements which describe the action or characteristics of a divine messenger or deliverer; such passages are now summed up in a title. The 'rule of God' may once more be instanced as an analogy. This abstract phrase is only seldom used for the kingdom of God, while in the Psalms the cry 'Yahweh is king' is often heard. But the Targum, the late-Jewish translation of the Old Testament into Aramaic, often replaced the verbal phrase by the abstract 'kingly rule' of God. The formation of the christological titles must be thought of as occurring in a similar way; they, too, were built up from biblical phrases.

The pre-Christian Jews already used the title Messiah = Christ. In the New Testament it is the central appellation of dignity, its primary position being explained by the messianic consciousness of Jesus, the trial and the crucifixion. The Messiah was an offspring of the house of David and hence *the* Son of David *par excellence*. The title Son of God and the two-stage christology, with the double sonship of Jesus, were derived from the prophecy of Nathan and from Psalm 2.7. Thus these three titles – Christ, Son of David and Son of God – are closely related; through the last two the Christ was more precisely designated; they pin-point the origin and the office of the king of the end-time.

Acts 2.30-35 and Hebrews 1.5 show that the Nathan prophecy was generally linked with Psalm 110, the two passages being associated according to the scheme of prophecy and fulfilment. Psalm 110 offered the title *Kyrios*: he who sits enthroned at the right hand of God in heaven is the 'Lord'. This title described the Messiah's warrant to rule: Jesus was set above the heavenly beings who pay homage to him as sovereign (Phil. 2.10 f.). He thus became as it were 'Lord of the spirits', a position which is reserved for God himself in the Similitudes of Ethiopian Enoch. Before Jesus' kingdom on earth can be established, it must be secured in the supernatural world, for the angels and demons are far stronger than any earthly power. On earth Jesus' sovereignty is for the time being known only to believers; consequently Jesus Christ is 'their Lord' (cf. Rom. 1.4). To the Jews, this is true of the royal rule of God, which already extends over all temporal existence, yet is recognized on earth only by Israel.

The Christians, celebrating the 'Lord's Supper' on the 'Lord's day', cried *Marana tha!* – 'Come, Lord!' (I Cor. 16.22; Rev. 22.20). With this call they besought the glorified *Kyrios* to come and establish his kingdom on earth, as Psalm 110 describes so powerfully. It will not do to deny the christological title 'Lord' to the Palestinian Christians and to say that it must have been devised in the Greek-speaking world. The very fact that the invocation 'Come, Lord!' has been preserved in Aramaic should be a warning here. Moreover, at this point the Qumran texts take us a step further. The old argument, still frequently met with today, that the form of address *mari*, 'Lord', is only used between people up to the third century AD, is never applied to God, and in consequence cannot have been employed for the enthroned Christ, is untenable.[20] For in the most important and extensive Aramaic document contemporary with Jesus, the 'Genesis Apocryphon' of Qumran, God is frequently extolled as the 'Lord of heaven and earth' (20.15), and 'Lord and ruler of the universe and all the kings of the earth' (20. 12-13; cf. 22.16, 21-22 and Dan. 2.47; 5.23). Moreover *mari* as a form of address also occurs in a prayer addressed to God (20.14-15) and the stereotyped opening of the Thanksgiving Hymns, 'I thank thee, O Lord', shows that 'Lord', the form of address used for God, must have been extremely common. Thus it was easy for the disciples to apply the title

[20] That Psalm 110 was not given a christological interpretation outside the Greek-speaking communities and the Septuagint version has been thrown into question by the Qumran fragment 11QMelch, published by A. S. van der Woude. This important text presupposes the enthronement of the archangel Michael as 'Melchizedek', the 'king of righteousness', and depicts his judgment on the devil and his spirits (cf. War Rule 17.5 ff.). The title 'Melchizedek' is certainly taken from the Enthronement Psalm 110.4, though the whole psalm, including the first verse used so often in the New Testament, probably underlies it.

'Lord', with which they had already addressed their earthly master, to the glorified Christ, especially as it precisely expresses the supreme power of the heavenly king.

The title 'Saviour' does not have to be originally attributed to the Greek church either. For the chief task of the Davidic Messiah of the Qumran writings is to 'save' Israel; that is especially brought out in the commentary on the Nathan prophecy. It is thus understandable that in the Gospels the motif of 'salvation' also appears. The angel in the Christmas story proclaims to the shepherds in the Bethlehem fields: 'To you (i.e. the representatives of Israel) is born this day . . . a Saviour' (Luke 2.11); and the Jews mock the crucified Jesus with the accusation that he wanted to be the saviour of Israel and could not save himself (Mark 15.31-32). Moreover, could it really have been the converted Gentiles who first discovered Jesus as Saviour? Did not the very name of Jesus, which means 'God saves', make it clear to the Palestinian Jews that Jesus was the Saviour?

'Son of Man', however, does not apparently fit into the framework of the titles grouped round the Messiah. How did it come to find an entry into the Gospels? Did Jesus perhaps describe himself as the Son of Man? And if so, what did he mean?

Ferdinand Hahn closes his investigation of the origin of the title 'Son of Man' with the sentence: 'Whatever may be the answer with regard to the roots of the concept in the history of religion, by New Testament times the idea of the Son of Man had long since become a particular element in the Jewish tradition and was at the same time to some extent a point of crystallization within the apocalyptic eschatological hope'.[21] But this statement cannot be substantiated. Hahn seems to be conscious of this, for in an extensive footnote he practically withdraws it.[22] In fact the apocalyptic

[21] F. Hahn, op. cit., pp. 21 f.   [22] Op. cit., p. 22, n. 1.

Son of Man, who is first mentioned in Dan. 7.13, is not an independent conception, nor is the term 'Son of Man' a title.[23] Furthermore, the use of the term is essentially confined to two writings: the Similitudes of Enoch and the Ezra Apocalypse. The latter of these two writings was compiled long after Jesus, about the end of the first century. The date of the Similitudes is a matter of doubt. A pre-Christian date is no longer considered certain, especially as, unlike the other books of Enoch, it is not represented among the fragments from the Qumran caves. In both the Similitudes and the Ezra Apocalypse the idea of the Son of Man is inspired by Dan. 7.13-14 and then worked out exegetically. In Daniel he is a mysterious figure appearing with the clouds of heaven. He is appointed before the throne of God to be the eternal ruler of the world; thus the succession of profane and tyrannical worldly kingdoms have reached their end. But 'Son of Man' is used in Daniel as an image. The writer simply means 'man', in contrast to the wild animals who are used as the symbol for the profane, anti-divine kingdoms. Later the concept is applied to a group, and explained as 'the people of the saints of the Most High' (Dan. 7.27). Admittedly the Similitudes and the Ezra Apocalypse do not follow this pre-existing biblical interpretation. They describe as 'Son of Man' an individual figure, Enoch transported to heaven or the Messiah coming from the sea. In these writings 'Son of Man' also simply means 'man' as opposed to other living beings. In Daniel 7.13 the 'Son of Man'='man' is contrasted with the chaos monsters, while in the book of Enoch, Enoch, transported to heaven, is called 'Son of Man'='man' to distinguish him from the angels (chs. 70-71). In all these instances the 'Son of Man' is the eschatological, true man, who has been chosen from the very

[23] So rightly N. Perrin, *Rediscovering the Teaching of Jesus,* London and New York 1967, pp. 164-73.

beginning, because he can stand before God and survive. This eschatological 'Son of Man'='man' corresponds with the original, primeval 'man'='Adam' or a righteous man like Enoch who had also been thought worthy of converse with God, face to face.

The Son of Man is entirely missing from the eschatological expectation of Qumran. God himself and the archangel Michael are the heavenly helpers of the godly; beside them there is scarcely room for a Son of Man, coming with the clouds of heaven. Yet the book of Daniel played an important part in the eschatological hope and the self-interpretation of the devout men of Qumran. It could be, however, that, in line with biblical interpretation, they saw the Son of Man in Daniel 7 as the 'saints of God', the community of the end-time, especially since they themselves intended to be those saints. Moreover, the Son of Man is missing from Pharisaic eschatology, for example in the Psalms of Solomon; even Paul, the former Pharisee and author of the earliest New Testament writings, never called the glorified Christ the Son of Man. He too no doubt interpreted the Son of Man in Daniel 7 as a symbol of the community of the end-time; this is indeed suggested by his pronouncement, 'The saints will judge the world' (I Cor. 6.2).

The point at which Jesus the Messiah was connected with the apocalyptic 'man' and at which 'Son of Man' became a title and a conception seems to have been primarily his glorification, his exaltation to heaven. As the Lord enthroned over the angels at the right hand of God, Jesus is a heavenly man. Since the Christians waited longingly for his coming as judge and ruler of the world, they now combined the picture of the heavenly Son of Man with the *parousia*. He will come as judge in the clouds of heaven to redeem the righteous and punish the disobedient. Like the title Lord, the appellation Son of Man is now used to interpret the messianic concept and to give it universal significance. There is a connection of this kind between Messiah and Son of Man in Mark 14.62, for example; in Matt. 19.27 the enthroned Messiah is replaced by the Son of Man. On the other hand, the invocation '*Marana tha!*' proves that even for the *parousia* hope the Lord, the Son of God, remained dominant, and not the Son of Man – as the earliest Pauline epistles show (I Thess. 1.10; 3.13; 4.15; 5.2; II Thess. 1.7-10).

The passages in which Jesus (referring to the lowliness of his earthly condition and the necessity of his passion) describes himself as 'Son of Man' may well be genuine. But it is not the apocalyptic Son of Man in Daniel 7.13 which must be envisaged as the prototype. Jesus uses this title, as a concealment and a revelation, to describe himself as the 'man' of the end-time, the 'man' after God's heart, who does God's will (cf. I Sam. 13.14 and Acts 13.22). This true, eschatological man is the king from the family of David, the Messiah before his enthronement. Like David of old he has already been anointed with the spirit of God and can therefore perform actions which bring salvation. Indeed, he challenges the devil because he wills to deliver Israel, not from its worldly enemies and the power of Rome, but from its sins and the rule of the evil one, and to win it for the kingdom of God (cf. Matt. 1.18). It is no coincidence that some of the sayings about the life of the Son of Man on earth recall the fate of David before he became king, misunderstood, hungry and without shelter (Mark 2.25-28; Luke 9.58). Jesus did not proclaim himself openly as Messiah; he simply called himself 'man', because this formal word remained ambiguous and mysterious and only made sense in the context of his work. The title 'Son of Man' offers no answer, but merely poses a question, like that provoked by the ministry of Jesus: 'What can this mean?' (Mark 1.27), 'Who is this man?' (Mark 4.41).

EPILOGUE: BREACH OR BRIDGE?

NO ADEQUATE answer can be given to the question of what we know about Jesus without consideration of the Judaism that lay behind him and the Christian church that was ahead. The thought and hopes of the devout Jewish community are the background without which the historical Jesus is obscure and liable to various modern misunderstandings. The Christian church, on the other hand, stands in the foreground, its creed at first blocking the way to the historical Jesus; and we are bound to test whether it simply conceals his intentions and work or is also an important indication of them. We have seen that the confession of faith is a genuine response to the work of the earthly Jesus; the messianic consciousness and the messianic secret of the Gospels are not artificial constructions. Indeed, the earthly Jesus and the Christ of the *kerygma* must always be seen together. The church did in fact see them together, expressing this by fusing the confession of faith 'Jesus is the Christ' into the name Jesus Christ. Kähler's distinction between Jesus the historical person and Christ the historical force may be a useful working hypothesis, but the strict either–or is untenable, both for the church and for the scholar. Without the historical Jesus the Christ of the church is hollow, a radiant shell, a mythical hero without historical weight. On the other hand, anyone who clings to the historical Jesus alone is blind, for without the light of the Easter creed he is swallowed up by the darkness of the cross.

The church of Jesus has no cause to fear the question of the historical Jesus. For its confession that Jesus is the

Christ is faithful both to the intention of Jesus and to the
action of God: Jesus' messianic claim was confirmed by
God when in the resurrection he created him Son and King
of the end-time. True, this is an article of faith – and the
church has to preach articles of faith. But it is not conjured
up out of nothing; it is based on history. It is the 'yes' of
faith to the claim of a historical personage. Apart from such
an assent there is only the decisive 'no' which is a denial of
Jesus' messianic claim. It is the 'no' of Caiaphas and the
Jews in Jerusalem. There is no third possibility. For whoever sees in Jesus the wandering rabbi, the proclaimer of
the end of the world or the witness of faith, falls short of his
own claim and the testimony of his disciples.

Certainly Easter is a new beginning, an eschatological
event which came about unexpectedly. But it does not represent a complete break with the story of Jesus. The idea of
the covenant may illustrate the way in which the relation
between old and new, continuity and discontinuity, should
be regarded. Just as the covenant which God will renew in
the Last Days may be called the New Covenant, although in
it the Old Covenant is established, so the resurrection of
Jesus is the establishment of the messianic dignity which
Jesus already possessed. Just as in Qumran the 'rise' of the
Messiah was longingly awaited, so the disciples who went
up to Jerusalem with Jesus hoped that he would 'rise' there,
be raised on Zion to the dignity of king of the end-time.
Arrest, trial and the cross killed that hope; it revived with
Jesus' resurrection.

Of course the messianic hope was now fundamentally
different; all dreams of national uprising and political rule
disappeared under the impact of the cross. It was only in
the light of Easter that the disciples understood Jesus' work
and intention: they now realized that the Messiah had to
undergo rejection and suffering, that he was to conquer not

Rome, but death and evil. We have no reason to mistrust the New Testament assurance. The Easter message and the historical Jesus are joined by a bridge resting on many piers. Jesus proclaimed the good news of the presence of God who, like a forgiving father, seeks his lost children and grants even sinners the company of the Redeemer; the disciples preached the Gospel of Christ, who appeared as saviour and died on the cross for sinners. In the Holy Spirit Jesus drove out unclean spirits and conquered Satan; from Easter onwards he was extolled as the Lord of all spirits, who gives the Holy Spirit to believers and in him is ever-present with them. Jesus was the representative of the Lord who forgives sins and heals all infirmities (Mark 2.1-12); the disciples acknowledged him as 'Lord' and transferred to him the position ascribed to the 'Lord' in the Old Testament. Just as Jesus placed the penitent heart and the saving will of God higher than the pride of the godly and the letter of the Torah, so Paul preached faith in Christ as the only way to salvation and rejected striving after righteousness through the works of the Law. Above all, Jesus knew himself to be the Messiah and he acted in messianic authority; hence the risen and glorified Jesus was acknowledged as the king of the last days. It is still faith, not sight, that is demanded from men. Just as the historic Jesus never acknowledged himself to the multitude as the Messiah, so the power of the glorified Christ is not visible on earth; only the disciples claimed to recognize Jesus as Messiah. But, as Jesus taught in a parable, that is a sign of the divine patience. For in the time of faith there is room for repentance, since each person can decide freely for Christ; in the era of sight, when the reign of Christ is manifest, only judgment is left for the undecided.

Why then did the Jews reject the proclamation of Christ? Was it not perhaps exaggerated? Did it not go beyond the bounds of the Jewish messianic doctrine? Who gave the disciples the right to sum up in Christ all the different heralds, helpers, saviours and judges of the Jewish eschatological hope and, later, to add Hellenistic redeemer-figures to the picture as well?

The Jewish hearers of the Gospel undoubtedly found themselves faced with a number of problems. They found the virgin birth an objectionable article of faith. For the Jewish Messiah can only be a son of God by adoption; he is anointed, not conceived, by the Holy Spirit. Moreover, the cross was for the Jews a stumbling block which even Easter could not entirely remove. For in place of the general resurrection of the dead there was now an individual, Jesus, who had risen from the grave; he was exalted to heavenly king without filling the position of earthly ruler. Death and evil were said to be conquered in the Christian *kerygma*, yet the world went on in its old way and mankind continued to suffer under sin and guilt, sickness and death. It was hard for the Jews to understand why the end of history should come about so secretly and hesitantly, with such long intervals.

Yet the link with Jewish faith is not lacking even here. In Qumran, for example, certain benefits of the messianic age were seen as present realities, although the great turning point still delayed. In the first place the saints, the eschatological community, already existed, even though in inconspicuous and incomplete form; and the people of Qumran believed that the heavenly saints, the angels, also went invisibly in and out of the camp, already realizing the communion destined to be visibly completed at the end of time. Moreover, the Qumran community was governed by the Holy Spirit (*Community Rule* 3.7), which at this time was held to be an eschatological gift; the speaker in the Thanksgiving Hymns thanks God especially for giving him the Holy Spirit (7.6-7).

But the form of this world will only change, or rather disappear, when the Messiah appears, conquering evil and beginning his sovereignty. Faith in Christ, drawing everything into its orbit, corresponds roughly to the hope which late Judaism cherished with regard to the end-time. Truth and justice will then break like a ray of light into the darkened world; everything which is not doomed to corruption springs up anew in fresh glory and unconquerable vitality, glorious as on the day of creation. The Messiah is the focus of this event. His victories reveal the divine power, his rule and judgment display the righteousness of God. Seen from this aspect, the claim of the proclamation of Christ is not surprising. If the Messiah had really come, if he had been enthroned as king by God, then the light of the last day was already shining in the world. Everything is new: belief in Christ inevitably includes a new, eschatological understanding of God, the world and one's own existence. The only question is how far the old divine revelation given to Israel is affected and re-evaluated by the eschatological interpretation of things. In Qumran the Law, as the essence of revelation, represents the constant. Just as in the end-time the Old Covenant will be finally established, so the Law, dictated on Sinai at the making of the Covenant, will be fully revealed. The end-time brings nothing fundamentally new, but renews the revelation which has already been given, revealing all its mysteries and imperfectly understood clauses. It is man who will be decisively altered, recreated and endowed with the insight of the heavenly beings. Even when Jesus and Paul give the assurance that they do not intend to abolish the Law but to 'establish' or 'fulfil' it (Matt. 5.17; Rom. 3.31), they really mean that in the end-time it will come fully into force and that men will then act according to the true will of God. But when Paul rejects obedience to the Law as the way of salvation and replaces it by faith in Christ, his position is unacceptable to the devout men of Qumran. True, in rabbinic circles it may occasionally be said that the Law will come to an end in the future era (Babylonian Talmud, *Niddah* 61b). Yet in the Qumran even the Messiah is subject to the Law – more, he even allows himself to be instructed in it by the priests. The Christ of the New Testament, on the other hand, is Lord over the Law. The earthly Christ showed that he could disregard the letter of the Torah. The glorified Christ is, according to Paul, the end of the Law, which is not a valid road to salvation because God will only justify believers; moreover, on the cross Christ lifted the curse which the Law imposed on sinners; finally, the whole of the Law will be fulfilled through Christ's gift of love. But even this breach which Paul, the former Pharisee, made with the Law once he had become a Christian is determined by the Jewish view of that Law. Because the Law counted as the way, the truth and the life, because it was extolled as the mediator between God and man, even as the pre-existent co-creator of the whole world, the Christian faith could not continue to exist side by side with an absolute Torah piety. Speculative obedience to the Torah and a consistently thought-out faith in Christ can certainly successively determine the existence of a person, but they cannot be co-ordinate powers; the history of Paul shows that clearly enough. Yet it was through this very struggle with speculative Torah piety that the Christian faith grew beyond the limits of the Jewish messianic expectation. Apart from Paul, that is shown by John the Evangelist, the second great New Testament witness to Christ; the thesis that the Law was given by Moses, but grace and truth by Jesus Christ (1.17), is one of the leading themes of the Fourth Gospel.

INDEXES

INDEX OF REFERENCES

I. Biblical

2. Qumran

GENERAL INDEX